*forks*
in the
*dishwasher*

# *forks*
## in the
# *dishwasher*

*a spiritual evolution*

VILATE BENTZ-BOLANOS

TATE PUBLISHING *& Enterprises*

*Forks in the Dishwasher*
Copyright © 2011 by Vilate Bentz-Bolanos. All rights reserved.

No part of this publication may be reproduced, stored in a retrieval system or transmitted in any way by any means, electronic, mechanical, photocopy, recording or otherwise without the prior permission of the author except as provided by USA copyright law.

This book is designed to provide accurate and authoritative information with regard to the subject matter covered. This information is given with the understanding that neither the author nor Tate Publishing, LLC is engaged in rendering legal, professional advice. Since the details of your situation are fact dependent, you should additionally seek the services of a competent professional.

The opinions expressed by the author are not necessarily those of Tate Publishing, LLC.

Published by Tate Publishing & Enterprises, LLC
127 E. Trade Center Terrace | Mustang, Oklahoma 73064 USA
1.888.361.9473 | www.tatepublishing.com

Tate Publishing is committed to excellence in the publishing industry. The company reflects the philosophy established by the founders, based on Psalm 68:11,
*"The Lord gave the word and great was the company of those who published it."*

Book design copyright © 2011 by Tate Publishing, LLC. All rights reserved.
*Cover design by Bekah Garibay*
*Interior design by Nathan Harmony*

Published in the United States of America

ISBN: 978-1-61739-909-1
1. Philosophy: Religious
2. Religion: Spirituality
11.01.25

# *Dedication*

Anica and Lucas, thank you so much for being my children. I love you more than words can express.

# Acknowledgments

Without Anica and Lucas, this book never would have come to be. It started as a letter that I wanted to tuck away for them but slowly began to feel like it had a purpose beyond their two sets of ears. They, along with Philip, my incredibly playful and supportive husband, are my greatest blessings. Thank you to my angel friends Brenda and Kristen for nonstop encouragement and inspiration. Much love and appreciation to those special family members who were first to read this. Your loving and honest feedback helped me more than you know. Finally, thank you to the universe at large, which I am grateful and blessed to be a part of. I know the inspiration comes from all that is.

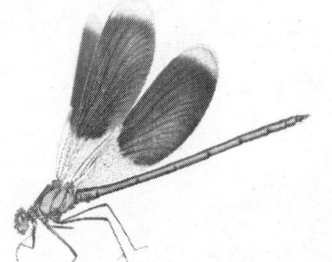

# Table of Contents

| | |
|---|---|
| The Forks | 11 |
| Mommy | 17 |
| Boxes, Labels, and Perspectives | 27 |
| Free Will | 39 |
| Decisions | 47 |
| You Get What You Give | 53 |
| Intentions | 63 |
| Unintentional | 73 |
| Making Room | 81 |

| | |
|---|---|
| The Bible | 89 |
| Control and the Mirror | 103 |
| The Scum | 111 |
| Death | 119 |
| Living Awake | 133 |
| Balance | 143 |
| In the Name of Science | 149 |
| My Science Report | 157 |
| Final Comments | 167 |

# The Forks

It seems funny that my spiritual evolution could be tied to the way one loads forks in the dishwasher, but it is. As you read this, it's important to remember this lesson first.

My mom taught me how to load the dishwasher. We pre-washed everything in hot, soapy water and then loaded clean dishes in the machine in a most organized fashion. I was taught to place all the forks upright in one compartment, all the spoons together, all the big spoons together, knives together, etc. We lined up the plates in neat rows. Yes, I still do load the dishwasher in the most organized fashion to facilitate loading the largest load possible. Mostly it just looks prettier that way. My mom, whom I was very close to and loved dearly, died five weeks before my thirteenth birthday. There's more on that somewhere in here ... but the lesson on the forks starts about two years later, when my stepmom, Jane, told me that I'd been loading the dishwasher wrong.

She said, "You need to separate the utensils so that they don't stick together and can get really clean." At first I was angry (yes, over forks), but I didn't express my feelings—especially anger—very well back then. It felt like she was saying that my mom did it wrong. For the next year, I would separate the utensils except when I was in this weird, ambivalent mood. On those occasions, I would put them all together.

It was years later, when I was living on my own, that I could see that they both were right. If I pre-washed the way my mom did, together was fine. However, if I did a quick rinse or stuck them in dirty, Jane's way was better. Separating them did get them cleaner. It's a big day when you realize that your mom was wrong about anything. I remember the day when standing at the dishwasher that I realized my mom was wrong about a few things, forks included. Wrong might be an incorrect label but maybe simply narrow or closed-minded in her thinking. Perhaps she didn't investigate some topics but just took what she was taught to believe as an absolute. Is that what happens when we're afraid to look at life for ourselves?

Please remember, no matter what I suggest, there's more than one way to load the forks in the dishwasher. Think big, investigate, question, examine, and see what feels true to you in your heart. There's always more than one path, one way to learn, or one way to answer the same problem. I want to pass along some of the things that I have learned. Some may work for you, and others may not serve you. *Take the pieces that fit and discard the ones that don't so that you can find other new paths for yourself.*

Throughout this book I have put a few things to consider at the end of each chapter. Whether you agree with me or not isn't the point. Think them through. Mull them over and give them a little consideration. Discuss them with a friend or write out your thoughts in the margins. It's your journey, and that's what matters.

The passion and energy of a parent, instructor, friend, or employer can make it hard to listen to your own voice and the messages that may be meant for you. As you read, listen to your own thoughts and feelings; be open to where it might take you. As I look back, I'm amazed at where my truths have taken me.

When I was supposed to consider something new or grow, the information came to me repeatedly and in a variety of ways. Have you ever seen a program on TV and then a month later had a friend bring up that same topic?

- Do you believe in coincidence? Could that layering of information be messages from your angels, guides, or God? Is it possible that you even set up certain situations for yourself as reminders?

- When you turned eighteen and registered to vote, did you pick the same party as your parents? If so, was this because they told you this was the "right side" or did you investigate for yourself? Did you just have a preference for elephants or donkeys? That's fine. Just realize that.

- What beliefs or truths of your own have you investigated? What have you taken from your mentors, clergy, or family? What have you discarded? Is there anything you have taken simply because it was what you were told you "should" believe? Can you think of anything you might have taken simply because it was your only exposure?

# Notes

# Mommy

They say that having children will change your life. Having children changed me. There are many things I have learned from my children. Perhaps one of the biggest was when I realized that all souls seemed to come to this planet with their own life plan, personality, and talents to help them achieve it.

For decades, psychologists have questioned whether *nature* or *nurture* was our biggest influence. Is it genetic programming that gives us our talents, personalities, and flaws? Is it the environment in which we were raised that becomes the main contributor to our skills, likes, and dislikes? I would imagine that in this day and age, most people agree that it's a combination. Is it possible that there's some divine design involved? Is it possible that our soul might have a specific thing that it wished to learn or experience? Would the universe or God then give us talents and skills to help facilitate that? Wouldn't we choose the parents or environment where we are most likely to get that experience?

My children, Anica and Lucas, are nineteen months apart in age. Their environment was identical. Philip, my husband, and I worked at the same places when each was born and actually still do. They ate the same food, were read the same books, saw the same TV shows and movies, and still proudly declare the other to be his or her best friend. Genetically speaking, they are both our biological children, so you would think they would have a lot of similarities. However, they are profoundly different from their personality to their daily habits to their skills and talents.

Anica is outgoing and eager to try everything from new foods to different instruments and sports to things like car racing and boating. She will be the first to raise her hand and offer an answer in class and doesn't mind being wrong. She enjoys being the center of attention and is very social. At three she began asking to go to dance class and start school "to make friends, Mom."

I couldn't believe that she felt ready to leave me, and it seemed too early for me. After a few months of her asking, I realized that she knew what she wanted and was ready. She never had a tearful moment. In her core she is social and a performer. She doesn't mind getting dirty, would run around naked if I let her, couldn't care less if her clothes matched, and could dance all day long. Anica has incredible compassion and has always been able to sense which kids are shy or need something, and will go out of her way to nurture them. She is more emotional, volatile, and more challenging. School doesn't come super easy for her, and she pretty much hates homework, especially spelling. After I read a book that encouraged me to consider what our soul's life plan is, it was obvious to me that she is here to explore and experience as much as possible.

I would describe Lucas's overall temperament as easygoing yet persistent and pure sunshine with brief periods of worrying. He was two when we were putting together some project, and he asked where the directions were. Even if he couldn't read them, he wanted to look at them before we started anything new. My "I'll consult them if I need them" attitude really seemed to bother him. He never likes to be first and prefers to sit back and watch someone else try and will then decide whether or not to give it a go. Trying new things is difficult for him. He loves to read and learn, and, yes, he likes homework. It's like he was a scholar before he got here. He's full of energy and athletic but is a homebody, unlike his "where are we going today" sister. Also unlike Anica, he will promptly wash his hands or shower if he gets dirty. He's quite proper, particular about his clothes matching, and is very modest. He even insists on wearing a swim shirt when swimming and is slow to warm up in new places. Lucas is rarely sassy like Anica can be and not as outwardly compassionate, but he's very thoughtful and considerate on a more personal level.

Of course some differences may be due to birth order, genetic pairing, and gender, but how much? Wouldn't you choose those things too? If not you, then wouldn't God choose that to give you a specific experience?

Once I understood that they were born that way for a reason, it made it easier for me to accept them the way they are. I no longer try to get Lucas to "jump in" and can respect the fact that he needs to watch first. I don't push him as hard to try new things and let him come to it on his own. That hasn't always been easy for his dad and me. I have found that he usually just needs a little time. The more we push, the more he resists.

I am also more patient when Anica wants to put on the show for us again and again. I get it now; that's who she is. As parents we want our children to conform to our house, our rules, our personality, and our philosophy on pretty much everything. We do that so much that sometimes we squash who they are. Anica's performer nature was hard for me at first. I wanted her to love reading like I did and, although I appreciated that she was so outgoing, worried that she should "tone it down." Looking back I see that I was trying to change that about her because it wasn't me. I'm not a big performer and don't care to be the center of attention, so her bringing that to the family was a process. I would have been a terrible mom for Jim Carrey or Robin Williams. I cannot even imagine trying to let those two live their personalities as little boys.

Of course that doesn't mean I let them have their own way on everything, push the limits, or completely cater to their personalities. I realized, however, that they are already their own people, in addition to my children. I hope to help them throughout the life *their* soul intended, instead of the one I might think is best.

The other way parenthood changed me was in my desire to be the best version of myself I could be. They absolutely have their own distinct personality and soul plan, but they learn how to handle the day-to-day stuff by watching me. It's easy to see when your child mimics and repeats your own words back to you. Doesn't it always sound so different to hear your words, tone, or see your mannerisms from them? Is it possible that our children come to us when they do to teach us something? Don't they remind us of the beauty and joy that is possible? Could they teach us as many things as we teach them? I certainly love the way they are so present in this moment, where my head is usually in the future, planning for this or that.

My spiritual path started evolving and changing a decade before they arrived. But it was watching my children's growth and curiosity that inspired me to write down these thoughts. Anica and Lucas have been the most incredible blessings of my life and have taught me more than I could write in any book. When I take the time to listen, they often surprise me with their wisdom, presence, and perceptiveness. One of the greatest gifts they gave me was when they started asking questions.

"Where did the very first baby come from?"
"Could we come back as a hamster?"
"Why did God create the universe?"

Sometimes I would tell them I needed a few minutes to put my answer into words. I told them from the beginning, "I don't have all the answers." But I could tell them what I thought. You have to be clear in your head to articulate answers aloud. Or at least I did. Their questions encouraged my clarity and kept my growth fueled.

I don't want to give the impression that I'm something I'm not. I get frustrated when the house seems destroyed only hours after I've cleaned it up, and I don't like it when they scream across the house for me. Like all parents, some days are great, and some are really a challenge. The best days seem to be when I can keep the presence of mind to not get too caught up in the little stuff and find that version of myself that I really like.

What if instead of a child's chore chart that said:

1. Make your bed
2. Feed the dog

3. Brush your teeth
4. Take out the trash
5. Wash your face

They had one that said:

1. Remember your spirit by saying prayers and thank yous
2. Remember your family by acting with love and respect
3. Remember your body by exercising to be healthy
4. Remember your mind: read, learn, and think big every day
5. Remember your heart by doing an act of kindness
6. Remember life is a gift and a blessing by doing something fun

Do you think they would still learn to brush their teeth and be clean by your example? What if you mixed the lists? What would the second chart teach your children that the first list doesn't?

What would schools look like if the emphasis shifted to grading on the child's ability to reason, share, exhibit kindness, compassion, go beyond tolerance to acceptance, problem solve, compromise, or negotiate? What if we asked them to look at world issues and see what their ideas were to improve them? Do you think we would be surprised? How would a change at the educational level change the world?

# Notes

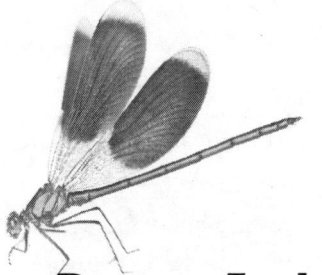

# Boxes, Labels, and Perspectives

Can you recall the last time you filled out a form for school, a doctor, or to apply for something? Can you remember all the boxes you had to check? Male or female, married or single, children, working full or part time, Caucasian, Hispanic, level of education, income, etc. I really have begun to dislike those boxes. Businesses chalk up an entire person's being with little boxes. Is it possible that people do that too?

In Anica's first year in dance, I met a woman who was new to the area. I tried to be friendly and chat with her. After asking me what I did and learning I was a nurse, she asked me if I could recommend a pediatrician. I started going through the names of local MDs who were thorough, skilled, and had kind bedside manners. When she said she wanted a woman for sure and Hispanic would be best, I must have looked puzzled. She looked at our daughters and said, "Well, they are minorities." She proceeded to explain how this would negatively impact them and make their lives harder. She theorized that a female, minority physician would understand our little girls on a deeper level and therefore be best. I sat there stunned and rather quiet. The idea that my daughter was a minority seemed foreign to me. The notion that this might make her life more of a struggle seemed unreal in this day and age.

I realize that we need adjectives in any language and that we need labels to distinguish me from you in conversation and in writing. However, there is a by-product that occurs from all these check boxes and labels. It seems to have become another way that we say, "I am separate, different, better, or worse than you." Think of all the labels that you have been asked to check in a box to describe yourself. Do they really sum up your personality? Is it even possible to sum up someone's soul? It's funny that we have all these adjectives to describe beings that are physiologically more than 99 percent the same. Where are the boxes that ask us all the ways we are alike?

One day, the elementary school sent home a form from the district, wanting to know the ethnicity of Anica and Lucas. They had several choices of different Hispanic or Asian origins, as well as more than ten nationalities. My mom had always told me, "We're Heinz 57, a little bit of everything." I grew up not really understanding what this meant, but was finally told just to check the Caucasian box. I stared at the kids' form and just felt irritated, which promptly turned to insulted and then indignant. Did they want to make judgments about the likely success of the students based on race? What possible purpose could the school district have for wanting to know that? Was funding of some kind based on that alone? *Is this legal?* I wondered. Where was the box that said, "decline to answer"? Surely if the Fifth Amendment meant that I could refuse to answer in court then I could refuse to put my children into a check box. In the end Philip and I wrote in our own check box and labeled it *American*. That was the only box we checked before signing and sending it in. Why does it matter where someone's distant family came from? Does someone's ancestral heritage make a difference to you? Why? If we really can agree that our skin—the package—makes no difference, why do we still ask? If we are still asking, isn't someone still making some judgment about the responses? Is someone still trying to say this group is better, smarter, worse, etc?

Think about the labels you gave yourself. If you divorced, would you still be you? If you dyed your skin blue, would you still be you? If testicular or breast cancer required that you have those body parts surgically excised, would you still love or hate chocolate or dogs or rain?

We put so much stock and make so many snap decisions because of the little boxes we see in ourselves or in other people. That mom in dance class had already decided that her daughter needed to be tougher than other girls and was going to have to fight for what she wanted in life because of the boxes she mentally checked for her. She gave those labels great power and impact in her and her daughter's future. I wonder how many people are stuck somewhere in life either physically or emotionally because of the power they have given a check box or a label of some kind.

Recently I was trying to explain to Anica the adage "Don't judge a book by its cover." Someone had told her that certain clothes make you more powerful and that people won't mess with you if you are wearing the right outfit.

I picked up her *Junie B. Jones* book (by Barbara Park) and asked her to tell me about the main character. We decided that Junie was smart, pretty sassy, but also funny.

I put another piece of paper over the cover and said, "Tell me about this book now."

She was puzzled and said, "It's the same book, Mom," with a look on her face that seemed to say, "Duh, I thought you were smarter than that."

"How about now?" I asked, swapping my quick-made orange paper cover for a blue one.

"It's still the same book," Anica said.

"So Junie B. is still smart, sassy, and funny?" I asked, and she nodded.

I asked her to tell me about herself. This actually stumped her for a moment, so I prompted her and told her some of the ways I see her and asked her to agree or disagree.

"I think you are smart, honest, kind, loving, a great big sister, a wonderful daughter, and occasionally cheeky. You have your daddy's ornery, playful streak, and you love to dance and sing."

She agreed and was able to add a few more.

"Are you those things in your pajamas?" I asked, and she said that she was.

"Are you those things in school clothes?" I asked again.

"Yes." She could see that.

"Are you those things naked?" This made her laugh, but she agreed that even naked she had those attributes.

"Are you those things whether I call you Anica or Angel-girl? What if I call you sweet cheeks or make up some other name for you?" I wanted to remind her that she isn't any label or adjective. *We're all something so much greater than that.* She agreed that she had those same attributes no matter what she wore or what someone called her. She said she knew who she is can only be found "on the inside."

I have one friend who says she puts on a suit when she has an important meeting because it makes her feel powerful. My sister will dress up and wear beautiful shoes to business events or meetings because it makes her more confident. Is there really power or confidence in the clothes? Is it possible that the clothes help them to tap into a specific energy or create a perception in their minds that draws out or projects those emotions?

Anica had it when she said who she was could be found "on the inside," but it's even deeper than our personality. The crazy thing is we sell ourselves so short when we only see the check boxes or labels. Yes, you sell everyone short when you deduce them to a few mere labels, but you sell yourself really short if that's all you see. I heard this great saying a few years ago: "God is like the ocean, and we're all a cup of that water." What if we made a conscious decision to see the part of God in each person? What if we really looked?

We've all judged a book by its cover, summed someone up in a few check boxes, or got mixed up in the right/wrong, good/bad of ethics, politics, office dramas, or societal values. Likewise, I know most of us have been on the other side of that equation. We've had someone stereotype, or make incorrect assumptions about who we are based on a superficial glance or label. The check box/label is really only superficial data. Do you suppose that your side of any argument is really the whole truth? Could that be superficial too? We get caught up in things being good or bad, right or wrong. Although this is different from the labels that we check off describing our status and bodies, it seems like a label to justify our viewpoint.

What does *wrong* really mean? We consider using racial slurs wrong, but sixty years ago it was common and accepted. We consider slavery wrong, but only a few hundred years ago it was considered a God-given right. I look at the issues that have flip-flopped on society's value of right and wrong in this short lifetime of mine alone, and it shocks me: homosexuality, interracial marriage, divorce, and being pro-choice are issues that seem more accepted today than twenty-five years ago. Likewise, corporal punishment and smoking both have negative connotations that weren't present two decades ago.

Is it possible that the right and wrong that people will vehemently argue, wage war upon, or declare lifelong feuds over are really sort of an illusion too?

What would happen if we could remove all our labels and erase every check box on the planet for a few days? Would the world look different? Would some people feel freed by this? Would some people feel a loss of status or identity without their labels?

What if instead of being motivated by the right/wrong, good/bad of a situation, we simplified it to look at our goals? What if instead of getting too emotionally bound, we stepped back in those times when searching for an answer and asked ourselves, *What is the goal related to this event, and does this help me reach it?*

When I simplified things this way, it felt easier to say "no" (this can be hard for us people pleasers). Working late or extra wasn't consistent with my goal of being a mom first. What if instead of going to a party with dread because you didn't really want to be there, you went with the mindset that you were going to stop by because it was consistent with your goal to maintain closeness with those involved. I know it sounds simple, but removing the labels allowed me to set boundaries more easily, honor my choices, and not feel guilty with the choices I made.

I started trying to use this reasoning with Anica and Lucas. I re-framed for them: "Did grabbing that toy get you what you wanted? Does pushing her ever work? Does throwing tantrums ever get you what you want?"

After a time-out, we would talk about what their goal had been. Did their way work or not? What else could they try next time that might help them achieve their objective? I admit to using the label "wrong" a lot when they were really little, but I found it hard to explain in that moment. I hope that they remember the talk after the time-out more than the label that put them there.

- What labels do you notice your friends using? What labels would you use to describe yourself? Do those words do you justice? Picture a person who doesn't like you. What labels would they use to describe you? Do those do you justice?

- If you could make up a check box form to gauge your success and happiness in life, what would those boxes be?

- How much of that data in those check box forms seems like a false or shallow representation of who you really are?

- If we agree that things like clothes have no real power but perhaps change our energy that we put out, could the same be true for the lucky rabbit's foot, the four-leaf clover, or a cross? Could the power of our talismans be the power they bring out from within us?

# Notes

# Free Will

I believe there are certain events in this life that we're destined to have, but that free will is the fundamental principle of this existence. It's the greatest gift because it allows us to create our own life and to live it. Have you heard the saying by Teilhard de Chardin? "We are not human beings having a spiritual experience. We are spiritual beings having a human experience."

Imagine yourself in your spirit form or in your version of heaven. As a spirit it must be easy to intellectually understand the concepts of hot and cold. But to feel cold water when you jump in the pool on a late fall day or immerse yourself in the warmth of a hot, relaxing shower is different. The feeling of being in love, making love, hugging your children, rain on your face, the freshness in a soft breeze, the smell of the ocean or fresh cookies, joy, and laughter are extraordinary moments that we get to feel, initiate, give, and be part of while in these bodies. Even feeling grief and sadness would seem like an honor and a great opportunity, I imagine. Think of how the contrast of cold makes warm feel so good and how when in the midst of loss we let ourselves dwell in the appreciation and love of those still present. We all can imagine many different events and circumstances but agree living them is different.

I believe our souls come here to enjoy, experience, feel, and grow or evolve. Some of our greatest moments for growth come when we decide how we're going to respond and what we're going to create when those predestined events happen in our life. It's always our choice (free will) how we react to things. Of course there's an emotional part, and this is important too. It's a big part of our understanding, learning, and it's often the catalyst to bring growth. If you never encountered a hard time, a struggle or pain, how would you have grown? As parents we tell our children, "That's hot. Don't touch." Most of us understood the concept at a very young age, but hasn't every one of us tried it until we got burned? The idea alone wasn't enough to teach us; we needed the experience to really learn.

I felt like my heart had been ripped out when my mom died, and I grieved for a long time. To this day, over twenty years later, I occasionally have tearful moments. If you live even a short time, you will feel the sorrow in some type of loss. Have you ever known someone who got stuck in that loss? Maybe he or she was never able to take a step back and heal. Instead, he or she gave up his or her free will and allowed the pain to grow to anger or bitterness. We have probably all been momentarily stuck there but may be able to recognize it better in a friend who never got over that divorce, job, girlfriend, etc. We love that friend so dearly, identify with his or her hurt, and feel bad with and for him or her, maybe even for years. We want them to heal but, from our little bit of distance, can see that the buried pain and anger will not allow it to resolve. I'm sure there are many reasons why people live in this state: inability to see they are stuck there, fear of looking at the past, reluctance to work through emotional pain, and certainly anxiety that they could be hurt again are only a few of the things that keep people trapped.

I have two friends who outwardly show their scars and anger toward events that happened to them more than twenty years ago, though I doubt they realize it. There's no question that hurtful or terrible events change you, just like my mom's death and my divorce changed me. We will all have things happen in this lifetime that are devastating, scary, hard, and painful. The gift of free will is that you can choose how they affect your future. You can choose to hold on to those difficulties and keep them alive by revisiting them in discussions with friends or keeping reminders.

For me to let go of the grief from my mother's death and the pain I felt when I divorced, I first had to acknowledge it. That was harder with my mom because I had locked things away and felt numb for the first few years. I wrote about my thoughts and feelings, which helped.

After my divorce I found that I had to let go of physical reminders that re-opened my hurt when I looked at them. Seeing the beautiful, brown, leather jacket from my ex-husband's mom in my closet every day made me sad and caused my brain to start down that memory path. Once I had acknowledged what I felt, I realized that I had to make a conscious decision to release it all. Part of that included that jacket. I tried it on one last time, let tears flow as I felt how much I missed him, all the dreams and plans that I'd had in that relationship and with that family. I made some peace with myself in that moment and then gave the jacket to a friend who lived out of town.

I wrote out ten things to be grateful for every day. In my sadness and depression, it wasn't always easy to find ten; often my number one was my dogs or a beautiful flower I'd seen. I made myself look for at least one or two new things to put on the list every day. Despite the struggle to find them, it helped me focus outside myself. I listed all the positive things I'd learned and gained from that relationship and those that I felt I'd given. When I was ready, I gave a lot of thought to what I really wanted to choose with my free will. I evaluated my jobs, how I spent my free time, and finally, I considered my relationships. I asked my sister how not to be a woman who repeated the same relationship over and over. She suggested I make a list of what I wanted in a partner and said, "When you start trying to justify why someone doesn't meet those things on the list, consider it a red flag."

There are many paths to freedom from the hard times and memories; you get to choose when and how to do it. Find what works best for you: write it out, talk it out, and seek out friends or experts to help you, but please, consciously choose. Don't let past events re-victimize and hurt you again and again. You can choose to give those memories power or to create something better and positive from them. Living with the ghosts and hurt of the past seems a tough road to choose.

Once you are clear that you're ready to let it go, stop rehashing the negatives with friends. Ask them to help you see the lessons and wisdom you learned and dwell on the positives that came from it. If there is absolutely not even one good thing, it made you stronger. It made you who you are, and without that the potential of who you can become would be different. You survived! If you choose to thrive, then you are victorious.

I can look back at my own family's weird dynamics and feel grateful because I am independent. It gave me the capacity to be both strong and sensitive. My dad gave me a few pearls of wisdom and knowledge. He also provided the *Bernstein Bears* example of parenting for me (what not to do). I'm a better mom because of that.

You know that saying "There is beauty in all things"? Maybe the true meaning is that there's a positive purpose, a gem of knowledge or an opportunity to experience in all things.

- Does God need anything from us as individuals? If God needed us to serve him or required specific things from us, would that contradict your notion of free will?

- Do you think we were a spirit before this body, or just after? If you believe that we have free will as a human, do we have free will as a spirit?

- What if, as free will implies, we get to choose our experiences, our paths, or our destiny? Perhaps predestined things happen to round out our experience? Is it possible that we choose some of those events in spirit form?

- If as a spirit you wanted to experience and feel forgiveness, wouldn't you need someone to forgive? Is it possible that the people we perceive as our enemies are truly our closest spiritual friends who have agreed to help us gain a certain experience?

# Notes

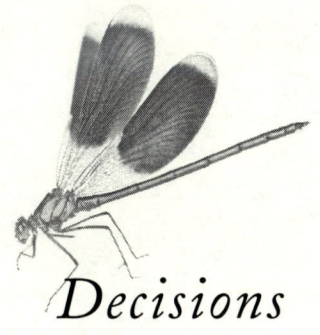

# Decisions

Why is it that when you make a decision, suddenly the grass looks a lot prettier on the other side? It makes you question your decision and yourself. Whether it was a decision to end a relationship, take a different job, move to a new area, try something new, or stay where you are, you have most likely ended up with the "what ifs" and remorse. Perhaps you make a decision to work part time to be with family and then a wonderful full-time job comes along. You feel tempted and question why the job of your dreams is coming now. Is it a sign that you were supposed to work full time again?

When I was young I believed these events were part of the temptations the Bible warns about. For a while I thought that when the fork appeared in the road, it was Satan trying to tempt me. Over time my thoughts changed, and I came to believe something completely different.

When you make a decision in your head, you feel good about it. There's a sense of resolution and peace with it. What if life/God/the universe is simply giving you the opportunity to stand up in action for your decision? Just like as a spirit, you understand cold, but as a human you get to feel it; it's one thing to know that decision in your head but a gift to get to live it. Ever have that big talk with yourself about your priorities? Before you know it, there's the opportunity to stand up, experience, and express what you had decided in your mind.

My mom used to tell me, "Don't play the 'what if' game. It's going to drive us both crazy!" I'm not talking about daydreaming, "What if I win the lotto tonight?" Nor am I talking about having a back-up plan or seeing red flags. I think it's smart to look at options when you see the signs of big change coming. If you know your company is downsizing and you're the newest employee hired, then it's prudent to start saying, "If it's me, I'm going to do X, Y, and Z." The "what ifs" I'm talking about are the ones where your hands sweat, your stomach aches, and you lose sleep. They are the things you generally have no control over. What if a bomb goes off here? What if my house gets broken into today? What if I get in a fight with Samantha at work? What if the kids' bus crashes today? What if I don't get the promotion? What if I don't get that job? You can spend an enormous amount of time and energy feeling anxious over the "what ifs." Does that angst ever change the outcome? Have you ever seen or even heard of a situation when worrying or looking at every possible bad "what if" altered the way it played out?

If it isn't that "what if" feeling but you truly think you followed the wrong fork in the road, remember that you have free will. You get to choose. You don't need to buy into the "I should stay at this job...with this person...in this house...because it's the 'right' thing to do." Start over, remove the labels, and ask yourself, *Does this help me get to my goal?* If not, change it.

What if there's not some terrible temptation that you must fight to understand, decipher, or interpret? I believe there's simply the opportunity to live your thoughts and priorities. I'm not minimizing that tough decisions come along and that there will be hard and painful events to deal with. I want you to feel a sense of empowerment that you can choose how you're going to respond to these challenges and shape the future you want.

- What if you tried to look at decisions from your spiritual side, not just your human side? Imagine yourself as a spirit, free of all the feelings of obligation, perhaps as a casual observer of your life instead. Does that perspective offer you any different insights?

- As you look at decisions, remove the labels, consider your own free will, and see if you change your thoughts on any of your routines or relationships. Are you still going to that specific church because your mom thinks you should? Did you stay an extra year or two in that past relationship because you felt obligated? Are you taking lessons or classes for yourself or because of another reason?

- If you can play with the idea that you are indeed the star of your life and your choices create your destiny, what do you choose to keep and what do you choose to discard?

- Do you suppose that life could be so much simpler than we make it?

# Notes

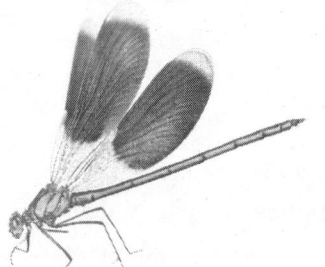

# *You Get What You Give*

Throw a rock into a lake, pond, or bathtub, and what do you see? Ripples; maybe small waves are formed depending on the size of your rock. If you were to watch closely, you'd see those ripples get smaller and smaller as they reach for the shore. You can see them far beyond what you expect when you really watch.

When we touch someone with love, respect, or kindness, our actions are like the pebbles in a pond. The people we touched are uplifted and will turn around and pass it along—maybe simply because they'll be in a better mood, or perhaps their energy is altered. Likewise, when we act unkindly, with revenge or malice, the person who receives that energy from us will be impacted from it and is likely to pass that on.

When I first read this, it was like a lightning bolt. I thought, *That's it. That's what I want my life to be about.* I never wanted to be famous or memorialized in history books. If I can be a lot of positive vibrations or ripples to affect the people around me in that way, then I knew I would feel proud of my life. As the years passed, I came upon a saying that explains why this works: "You get what you give."

This has been a wonderful concept to learn and to teach Anica and Lucas. Why is this so cool? What things are in your control *all the time*? The energy you give, the way you react to things, and the decisions you make. The amazing thing about that transfer of energy is what you decided to give comes back to you from those around you. If you are a helpful, loving, honest, and respectful person, that's what you will get back and attract in the people in your life, and it's the way others will treat you

It's true that sometimes a person's negativity will collide with you: that person with road rage who yells at you, that distracted mom at the store who crowds you in line, and of course those friends stuck in patterns of negativity. You can realize and choose to pass that on, or throw a new pebble and create a new wave of energy. I've told my kids and a few coworkers that a squabble takes two. Either person can stop reacting, and the issue will be over. At any point, in any situation, you can throw a huge rock and make a bigger wave.

This was my first exposure to what's now commonly called the "law of attraction." Most people believe in this, even if unconsciously. They will say with confidence, "What goes around comes around." "You reap what you sow," and biblical sayings like Luke 6:31, "Do unto others as you would have them do unto you," are widely accepted as an inherent truth. To me, this is the basic foundation for the law of attraction.

Keep in mind that if you give something with the intention of what you're going to get back, then what are you truly giving? Those are thoughts and actions based in our own selfishness or ulterior motives, and that's what we will get back: others' selfishness and ulterior motives. This might sound tricky because sometimes we have more than one motive—we want that job to help others and also to make money, or we want to do a favor for that friend because it benefits us too.

The best way I have found to honor and ensure my intentions are above board and where I want them is to be honest all the time, even when it's hard. I want to be honest about myself, honest about my relationships with others, honest with everyone. Then at a minimum, I feel good about whom I've chosen to be, and I know that honesty will come back to me. Besides, being untruthful simply doesn't work. It may briefly avoid confrontation or obtain a goal, but it will most likely cause you considerable stress and discord. Like the sunshine, the truth always comes out.

When those pre-planned life events happen, we utilize our free will to determine how we're going to react and what we're going to create out of those big events. What are we doing with our free will the rest of time? I think this is where the law of attraction really integrates into our daily lives. It goes deeper than just our thoughts, in part because the energy of our thoughts is more powerful than we realize. Remember the *Little Engine That Could*? It's the repetitive thought, *I think I can, I think I can, I think can*, that helps it over the hill.

What do you draw to yourself on a daily basis? We all have this voice in our head. When we don't like our reflection, it says, *I'm ugly*. When we're worried about a test, it says, *I can't do it*, and so on. I once read an analogy that explained the universe as a giant copy machine ready to duplicate and bring you the experience you're telling it to copy with your thoughts. If I sit there thinking, saying, and feeling, "I can't do it. I'm going to fail my test," over and over, then that's what our mind and the universe gives me: a mental block, anxiety, and a poor test grade. If I say, "I don't want to hurt, I don't want to hurt," then that's the experience it gives me—not wanting to hurt anymore.

I think that this happens both physically and perceptually. If you say, "My family is so full of drama. Ugh, my family is so full of drama," then first and foremost, that's what you notice—the drama. The more you "notice," the more you get sucked into the drama, carry it with you, and become involved with it. Things grow with attention, so of course the drama grows. Why not try saying and noticing, "Life is so much fun, my life is joyful, and my life is awesome." Say it in your head, tell it to your kids, write it in your journal, and see if it becomes more fun. Make sure that your words are honest. When you're in the moment of anger or despair, and you say with doubt or begrudgingly, "I'm happy," your words are weak and limited. Maybe it's like a copy machine without ink or toner. I know sometimes you will struggle to muster up a positive feeling to match with your words. For myself, "speak it, think it, feel it," is the order I use most. Start with one and the others will follow.

For years as a nurse I would watch sick people struggle and say, "I can't breathe, I can't breathe," or "I'm afraid it's cancer, I'm afraid it's cancer," and indeed they always seemed to get more short of breath or a terrible diagnosis. How do you know if your problem is something drawn to you by your thoughts to the universal Xerox or one of those predestined events supposed to happen in your life? Although you might get a feeling for which one it is with a little introspection, does it matter? It doesn't. What really matters is what you're going to choose to do now.

This idea and the story of the *Little Engine That Could* emphasizes the importance of thinking positively, staying in that frame of mind, and surrounding yourself with people who help to keep you up.

It sounds pretty easy, but you will meet people who tell you, "It's too hard," or "It's impossible." If they believe they can't change their thoughts, then what message does that send to the copy machine? It must become "too hard." It was interesting to me when I learned that those negative, repetitive thought patterns come from a tiny piece of tissue—about the size of a pea—in our brain, mapped as the language center. It serves the purpose to tell stories and control language, but it gets carried away. Just like you can tell your brain, "Don't move my arm," or you can tell your bladder, "Hold it for a few more minutes," you can tell that collection of cells, "knock it off" or "I control my thoughts."

I went through a time where I would have really creepy thoughts. I developed a positive sentence, a mantra really. The second I realized those thoughts were back, I would silently repeat my mantra. I would say it a few times and then go focus on something or someone else. Rapidly, those creepy thoughts became less and less and quickly stopped.

Have you heard the story of the two monks? They're on a long walk and come to a stream where a woman was standing and trying to figure out how to get across without soiling her dress. One of the monks wordlessly picked her up and carried her across the stream, setting her down on the other bank. The second monk stared at his friend in disbelief. For the next few hours the friend wondered why the first monk would do that. Did he remember they were not to touch women? What could have possessed him?

How could he have acted in that way? Finally as they approached their destination, the friend said, "Why did you carry her across the river?" The first monk looked back at his friend and said, "You've been carrying her all this time? I set her down hours ago."

- What if everything started with a thought? Do you suppose a person ever became president without that very first thought, *I could do that, I could be president*? Do you suppose a person preparing to rob a convenience store does so without first thinking, *I could do that... I could knock over that place and get the money I need*? What could you create by channeling your thoughts?

- Is your body stronger than a TV? Is the combined energy of your body, mind, and spirit more powerful than a TV? If the TV can emit signals to the far depths of space, how far could your energy extend? What if you tried to focus your energy?

- Ever heard the saying, "people who have nothing to hide, hide nothing"? What if we were all transparent in all areas of our life? Do you think most of our struggles or experiences would feel the same? Circumstances would surely change, but fear, loss, grief, anger, pride, frustration, and love; would those feel pretty similar? What if we learned and taught each other from this? Would businesses be more ethical and honest if there was total transparency in their bookkeeping and business practices? Would your neighbor or mechanic feel trustworthy if they had this same kind of transparency? What do you think causes some people to be severely "private" people?

# Notes

# Intentions

My dad used to say that it takes twenty-one days to break a habit or to make a new one. When I was fifteen, I was sitting on the foot of my bed and feeling unhappy. I just didn't like myself very much. A thought came to me from out of nowhere and inspired me, "I could change me." I simply needed to decide what I wanted to be and which actions would be in alignment with those qualities. I could start doing those actions, and while it would seem unnatural and awkward for a few days, it would be a habit in twenty-one days. It would be who I'd become. It seemed an amazing thought that in just three short weeks, I could transform and consciously create the "me" I wanted to be.

When I was a little older and read about the messages we send the universe in the terms of the giant Xerox machine, my intention setting began to take another turn. Then not long after, I saw a segment on a morning show about how to help reduce anger in kids with impulse control or rage issues. The guest expert said to teach them to say out loud, "I am in control" or "I choose to be in control" for one minute and the rage would dissipate.

The concepts I was learning began to layer themselves upon each other. Each of them reinforced things I believed but opened my thoughts just a little bit further. A while after the TV segment, I read about a comic who used positive affirmations and how they worked for him in a *Reader's Digest* in some waiting room. As I contemplated the universe as a big Xerox machine, I began to think about consciously choosing myself again. Was it time to revise and redefine who I was? Who did I want to be? What kind of person did I want to be? I carefully picked a few characteristics and started. "I choose to be honest. I choose to be strong. I choose to be compassionate. I choose to be humble. I choose to be respectful. I choose to be responsible. I choose to be kind. I choose to be loving." I said them daily, after my prayers at night, when I was driving home, and especially when I wasn't feeling good emotionally. I will never forget, after my divorce, driving along the bluffs with tears streaming down my face, continuously saying, "I choose to be strong. I choose to be strong." I didn't feel strong at the moment, but I knew as I sent the message to the universe that it would come. As years have passed, I have added some and changed some. I have chosen to be a great mom, patient, a good listener, wise, or peaceful. I no longer say "I choose." Now I say "I am" or "I have," and I know that I'm creating when I do this.

Who do you want to be? If that question seems complicated, how would you want your friends or family to describe you?

Maybe you've been saying and writing all the positive things, but nothing seems to be happening right away. Haven't we all felt that God is ignoring our prayers at some point? Consider this: we all have many facets like a beautiful gem. One facet might be our words; other facets might be our actions, feelings, and thoughts just to start with. It strikes me how similar this is to the way we think of the Holy Trinity to explain a few facets of God. I've heard the Holy Spirit often expressed as the feeling of divinity, Jesus as God manifested in human form, and God as the pure, ethereal energy like our thoughts. Which of your facets do you want God/universe/angels to listen to? Thoughts this time, words next time? What happens when one facet, perhaps your words, don't match your emotions or actions? How do you get all of them to match? Does it matter which one comes first? Does one lead to another?

I read a study about two men who were mapping facial muscles and localizing which ones twitched or moved in various situations. For example, a genuine smile moved more muscles than a fake one. The researchers were incredibly precise and spent years studying the 1,500-plus different expressions we can make. At one point they realized they were becoming short with one another and had been feeling grumpy and sad. One of them became aware that they had been mapping and making the expressions associated with anger and sadness for a few weeks. This sparked another study. Could the expression trigger the emotion? What do you think those results showed? It kind of makes you want to start smiling, doesn't it?

It illustrates that no matter whether you start with thinking the happier thoughts, saying the positive affirmations, taking steps through your actions, acknowledging and focusing on the positive feelings, they all lead to one another. It's like you create a great circle; the more you do one, the more the others follow. The only important thing is to decide to start.

I believe the other part people struggle with is, "Okay, how long will it take?" I was particularly impatient about this before I realized that time is a divine blessing. Think back to the last time you experienced bad turbulence during a plane flight. For a few moments with incredible intensity, you and most of the other passengers thought, *Oh my God, we're going to crash!* You stiffened, gripped the armrests, and perhaps made a quick categorization of the life you were leaving behind. All the facets lined up in that moment of fear. An event like that or a horror movie that left us jumpy for a few days would do us all in! Our perception of time is another gift to prevent situations like those or impulsive, emotional intentions from occurring. It gives us the opportunity to make clear and thoughtful choices.

I read a book by Victor Wooten called *The Music Lesson*, which made me think about using time wisely. In this book, Michael, a spiritual guru music teacher, asks his student to consider how long a baby holds the intention of walking or speaking before they master those skills. He points out that every child surrounds his or herself by expert walkers and talkers to watch, listen to, and learn from. He further challenges his pupil to find ways to surround himself with experts in his music.

If these are new ideas and skills, can you expect to be great at it on your first attempt any more than a baby strides across the kitchen on their first attempt? Is it possible that there's a learning curve to everything? Could each book, free Internet conference, or DVD lecture be a way for you to surround yourself with experts to learn from?

- When you take the power of the sun and focus it through a magnifying glass, you can start a fire, fry an ant, or cause a burn on your skin. Could we be the magnifying glass? Could we focus the "sun" in ways we perceive as positive or negative?

- Do you remember that biblical passage that talks about "Whenever two or more are gathered in my name…"? Could we increase our energy or the power of our requests to God/universe/guides if we said our intentions with a friend?

- Is this why prayer chains/prayer groups work?
- At the last concert you attended, was there an energy you could feel in the crowd? What was it about the crowd that gave it that feeling?
- I once read that if you hold your focus and intentions on something that benefits you, you will harness all the incredible energy and power of your entire being to bring about that intention (like the magnifying glass). However, if you hold your focus and intentions on something good that benefits mankind, then you will harness all the energy and power of mankind to bring about that intention.
- Re-read that last sentence, and this time substitute "Leukemia Society" for mankind. When you are finished, try it again and substitute the name of your workplace or "the planet."
- Is this how individuals sometimes bring about great change or have an amazing impact in the world?

- Is a personal intention to win the lottery less powerful than a genuine act of kindness? I don't have all the answers, but it sure is interesting to consider.

# Notes

# *Unintentional*

"It's great to set your intentions for tomorrow, but don't forget to look at your life right now and see what intentions you've been setting." This was a quote I heard a while back, and it made me think about the unintentional intentions that I'd created.

At twenty-six I was diagnosed as having basal cell carcinoma (a very slow-growing skin cancer). This was nothing life threatening. It was more annoying than anything else. I had a large one on my forehead that had been there for more than two years that regular MDs had failed to label. I finally made my way to the dermatologist, who took one look at me and said, "What is a twenty-six-year-old doing with a basal cell?" I shrugged. These types of skin cancers are usually found in people in their sixties, seventies, and eighties.

Over the next few years, I had three surgically removed and one frozen off on my lip. Then there was the one that appeared on the left side of the bridge of my nose. The doctor was afraid to freeze it due to my previous scarring; he said there wasn't enough tissue there to cut it out without grafting and tried a variety of creams. They were supposed to slough off the tissue until the cancerous spot was gone. Four creams and three years later, the spot would look gone but would return.

I began to wonder if it came back because I expected it to. After all, the cells were all new. The body is designed with impressive regenerating abilities and an immune system that seeks out and eliminates foreign cells all the time. Perhaps it was coming back because I'd labeled myself as having basal cell. I saw myself in my head with them and quite simply, I expected them to be there. I asked myself if I was getting some payoff out of this, like people's interest or sympathy. I knew, if nothing else, it was time to look at all the variables.

One night I visualized the white blood cells going to the basal cell and tearing it down. I started putting vitamin E oil on it, which I had tried years before with no change. This time as I did it, I encouraged my body to heal. It flattened out and shrank by a third within a few weeks. Within a month it had almost vanished, but a week later it was there, smaller yet pink and present as ever. I began to think of it as my spiritual barometer. When I was visualizing its improvement, it did great; when I slacked off, it came back as a reminder. After six years of having it there and four months of concentrating on it, I decided I was ready to see it be gone but still wasn't sure how.

I went to the bathroom to have a talk with the basal cell. It sounds dumb, but I had tried everything else that I could think of. I focused my eyes in the mirror directly on the spot on my nose, letting the rest of my reflection blur away. I thanked it for all that it had taught me and the things that it reminded me to do on a daily basis. I told it, "It's time to heal up and be gone now." I explained what I would say to anyone who might notice it was gone, in some weird way, trying to validate the basal cell. Within four days it was gone. *Had I done it this time?* I wondered. For two weeks it was gone or somehow magically invisible. I tried to hold the vision of it being completely healed.

I kept feeling like I needed to hold that vision instead of just being grateful that it was gone.

What was I supposed to learn from this? I felt like if I could master my thoughts, I could take care of it. I later laughed at myself, thinking of all the attention I gave it. *I might as well have named it,* I thought sarcastically.

I wasn't sure if this was one of those things I was supposed to encounter or if I had drawn it to myself? Nor was I sure if I was supposed to handle this traditionally or spiritually. In the end I remembered that none of us has to handle anything alone or in one single way. We may choose to do that out of an independent (or stubborn probably, in my case) spirit. As an RN, my advice to anyone else would've been to use a multidisciplinary approach: a new dermatologist for a second opinion and treatment options, prayer, vitamins, touch, and visualization to adjunct the treatment. "Utilize all your options," is what I would have told anyone who asked me.

From the time I began studying as a nurse, it seemed that this approach made the most sense. No matter what the problem was—medical, social, parental, economic, emotional, or spiritual—my recommendation to loved ones and patients was always to use all available resources. It took a long, drawn-out battle of wills with a pink spot on my nose to remind me that my advice was good and I should take it myself.

I think we all unconsciously make choices from time to time. I also think that when things come up, we focus on there being only one way to solve the problem (just like thinking there's only one way to load the forks in the dishwasher). What if we remembered to utilize the power of our bodies and minds while we see our doctor, priest, therapist, etc?

We've all heard of people who beat the odds. They walked again after a doctor said they never would or recovered from terminal cancer. What attitude do you think they had? What message were they sending the universal Xerox? Do you think the paralyzed man who walked again was the one who visualized himself as cripple and was resigned? "Yeah, my doctor said I'll never walk again." Or the one who said, "I'll be walking out of this place!"

- If you can set intentions to alter your personality or your health, what intentions could you set to bring about your happiness, wealth, or security? How much of those are truly just perceptions? What's your real definition of success and happiness? I know I have a few superficial ones that quickly come to mind, but I know others are truer in my heart.

- Why do we seem to equate happiness with material things? What if you only had two choices: a happy life, renting an apartment, old cars, modest vacations, and joyful memories, or a big house, expensive car, nice clothes, full-time job, and debt? Why would you make the choice you did? Does the material stuff give a real or false sense of security or self-esteem? Is it a societal standard? There's no judgment here. I have a house and would love a new car, but sometimes I look back and wonder about the choices I made too. Did they complicate my life with more worry and debt? Why did I choose what I did?

- I think there are times when we are operating on our higher level. We're sure of ourselves and the intentions we're putting out. Are these the times we're aware of how connected we are to God or each other? Sometimes I have more patience, more ability to laugh, to be fun, to articulate well instead of getting frustrated. What if we could operate on this higher plane or be the greatest version of ourselves more often? How would that change our current situation or relationships? Would it simply make our lives more fun?

# Notes

# Making Room

A friend of mine wants to find someone to share her life with. She dated a man for two years, and, although they loved each other, there were some big barriers preventing their relationship from growing—a young child from a previous relationship and his inability to set boundaries with the ex. Although my friend loved him deeply, she realized she wouldn't be fulfilled always being second or third in that relationship and decided to end it. They haven't been together for nearly two years and rarely run into each other, but they text each other a few times a month. She feels lonely that she hasn't found a new relationship. It seemed like despite both of them saying they were done with their relationship, part of them was still reluctant to let go. I think the messages we send to the "universal Xerox," or God, can sometimes be tricky. Did she really want to find a new relationship? Did she want the old relationship to work but somehow be magically different? If you're still holding onto something or someone, then the feeling-message you're sending is, "I'm not done here." The Xerox goes to work and voila, you're not done.

Everyone has had someone ask how his or her day was, just to be polite. We all dutifully say, "fine," even if we're having the best or worst day of our life. We felt the insincerity and gave them the answer they were expecting. If we can sense that, then surely, on some unconscious level, we can sense when someone is open and ready to be in a relationship and when they're not. We might not articulate it but may have chalked it up to the chemistry not being there. Whether you are making room for a new lover, job, house, or new you, these ideas cross over.

How do you make room? Start by being honest with yourself about where you are and how you're feeling. Get clear about where you want to go. What does that look like in your head? Only imagine a great-looking model on your arm if you want someone based on looks. Why not imagine yourself happy, feeling cherished, spending without worry, being charitable, feeling in perfect health; whatever it is that you're looking for in your life. Don't limit yourself to physical characteristics; you know that the package is temporary, fleeting, and unimportant.

Remember that we all have free will. You can't wish or intend someone or something else to be different. However, every action causes an equal or greater reaction. Do you remember that principle from science class? As you begin to change and purposefully create your own happiness, your life, people, and circumstances will transform around you.

Next, be grateful for what you have. Nothing new can come into your life if the message you're sending the copy machine is, "Life sucks … I hate him … my job stinks … I'm miserable.…" Remember, that's what you will get back, more situations that are unhappy, yucky, or painful.

Let me tell you a story about the drawing effect of gratitude on a very small scale. As a kid when we saw gnats, my mom would tell me to pray for the dragonflies to come. They always did, and now they've become a special symbol for me. One morning, I was sitting on the back patio with Anica and Lucas. I saw a large blue dragonfly and pointed him out. I told the dragonfly out loud, "Thank you!" Within a few seconds, I saw three more, and I excitedly thanked each one.

"There sure are a lot of dragonflies today," I told the kids.

Anica replied, "The more you thank them, the more they come."

"That's a very wise thing you just said. Do you think that's true for other parts of your life?" I asked her. I was searching my memory, trying to remember if I had said that to her recently or if she'd come with that on her own.

"Yeah," she said, like it was totally obvious and no big deal at all. She was quickly distracted watering the potted plants.

Lucas and I continued to watch the dragonflies together. I thanked each one, blew kisses to others, and remarked on great flying patterns with Lucas joining in on my excitement. Every few seconds a few more blue and orange dragonflies would flit by.

"Wow, that's like twenty already," I said after a minute. I felt quite honored by their show. The dragonflies approached from the far west and dipped down into my yard, flying only a few yards from our chairs and perfectly at eye level. After they passed us, the beautiful little creatures would jet back up in the air and fly away to the east.

Over the next twenty minutes, we watched, blessed, and thanked more than 120 dragonflies, and that's a conservative count! Finally the phone rang, and my attention was divided. As we stopped thanking and noticing them, they stopped coming.

Be aware that the universe/God is talking to you all the time. If a book catches your eye, pick it up. When a friend says something to you that seems to mirror where you are, listen. If a stranger gives you advice, evaluate it. Some of my biggest "Aha" moments have come from the strangest sources. Be open to the ideas and solutions that the angels bring.

- Does everyone want the same thing? Does the kid in rural Africa want what a child in the Bronx or Santa Monica wants? What if you believed there was more than enough? Would you be inclined to share more? What if we took half of our excess and gave it away? What would that make room for in our lives? Someone once told me that Americans use approximately 20 percent of what we have. What do you do with your extra 80 percent? I'm sure mine sits and collects dust.

- It seems that the marketing industry tells us this one is "bigger," "better," "faster," "prettier." We buy into that so easily. When is *it* enough? When do we have enough money? Enough possessions? Maybe we should ask this of our entire planet.

- As "a nation under God," what if we committed to trying to meet the basic needs (food, shelter) of our planet's people? How would that change the way our nation is perceived? Would other nations rise to our standards of peace, diplomacy, and love? If three other countries followed our lead, would it be worth it? How would the world change?

- What if we just did what we loved? Would the rest follow?

# Notes

# The Bible

My mom watched very little TV, especially by today's standards. She did have two shows she enjoyed and watched whenever she could: *Perry Mason* and *Star Trek*. I remember watching with her, from time to time, on one of twelve (yes, only twelve) channels that were available on the cable television of my youth.

It was two decades later when my husband, Philip, and I were talking about God and different religions that he referenced one of the shows I'd seen with her. He was nervous I would think it was crazy that his beliefs had been influenced by a *Star Trek* episode. He explained Captain James T. Kirk had encountered this mysterious cloudy substance. The mist explained that it could have many faces. Although it had been called many things and was seen many different ways, it was still God. That rang true for him. I was stunned and amused to hear that my strictly Catholic-raised husband and I had seen the same episode in our childhood and somehow come to the same conclusion.

As a child I believed that the Bible was the only Word of God. With a pretty traditional, strict religious background, I remember scaring the snot out of two friends on my very first sleepover. I was worried and explained to them that if they didn't go to church and accept Jesus into their heart, they would burn in hell forever. They had nightmares after my visit; I was never invited back again. My mom sat me down to try to explain the line I had crossed, but I didn't understand. Naturally, I believed what my mother told me about everything, even when she said to be leery of Mormons, Jehovah's Witnesses, Dungeons and Dragons games, and things like tarot cards.

In my college sociology class, my professor worked hard to make the subject interesting. I can't tell you many details of that class, but some of the things we discussed impacted me deeply. As I look back, I realize that I cannot guarantee the accuracy of his statements or my memory of them. It's interesting how our teachers' and clergy's words can be so impactful, and we tend to give them great credibility. What he did do was open my mind to some very new thoughts on religion and the Bible.

One week we traced the world religions like a family tree, with each current denomination getting its own branch. I remember drawing the tree in reverse and was amazed by what we discovered. Although we drew the tree branches to trunk, I think I can explain the way I remember it better the other way around. The trunk split and became the Eastern and Western religions, with the Western branch becoming the Roman Catholic Church. As different groups within the church began to disagree over doctrine, there would be a limb off into a new religion. In fact, all the current religions came off those branches. I was floored to realize that "my religion" came from the same religious base as the Mormons, the Catholics, the Jehovah's Witnesses, the Presbyterians, the Lutherans, etc. *People* had disagreed and formed new branches, and that had nothing to do with God but more to do with personal interpretation than anything else. I was further amazed that the Eastern and Western religions, that seem so far apart, had come from the same base.

In another lecture we discussed how the Bible developed into its current translation. I recall this being the first time I had ever heard of the Dead Sea Scrolls or even really considered how the Bible came into being. Although I knew it had been translated, it never had occurred to me that it might have been originally written in letters or handwritten versions in multiple languages, including Arabic, Hebrew, and Latin. He said that in the early AD period, Roman leaders had asked families to bring in their handwritten versions of the Bible. For decades they read, sorted through, combined, and abridged the stories. Eventually *they* wrote what has become the standard text. People often forget that God and Jesus didn't write it; it was people, no doubt inspired to write down the stories passed down to them. He suggested that the New Testament, and later the Old Testament, had been revised to omit any references to reincarnation.

*Hmm, that's interesting*, I thought. As he spoke I could see in my mind a group of church elders sitting around a big table. Perhaps they decided to remove those sections because they felt if people believed in reincarnation they wouldn't live their best life. I could see how their intentions might have been good—

natured and surely they could've felt they were doing humanity a favor.

As the years went by, I read books by spiritual teachers, psychics, hypnotherapists, and participants of past-life regression to investigate this topic. I found information in a book by Brian Weiss, MD as to when those references were removed. His research concluded Roman Emperor Constantine the Great removed the references from the New Testament in AD 325. Two hundred years later in AD 533, the second council of Constantinople confirmed this action and declared reincarnation was heresy, ensuring that the remaining references to reincarnation were removed from the Bible (*Many Lives, Many Masters* by B. Weiss, MD).

This was such an unfamiliar concept to me. I'd been taught that the Bible was perfect, holy, and infallible. Even though reincarnation felt plausible, even likely, I had a hard time embracing it. My intent is not to convince anyone of anything. I just realized over the years that I knew very little about the book that was the basis of my faith. I hope you question, investigate, and have many great discussions on this that stretch your mind as you find your own answers. Doesn't the mere topic of reincarnation bring many wonderful questions to mind? If matter cannot be created or destroyed but changes form, could we? Clearly, I don't have the answers, but I feel that we have been here before in different bodies.

What if we've all been the man, the woman, had light skin and dark, every color of hair, and have lived in a variety of times and places? Does it seem logical that in billions of years, in all of eternity, we would only take one human form for a brief average of seventy years?

For several summers as a young girl, I attended a week-long church camp. One year I asked the counselors about my animals. I loved my dogs dearly and felt worried about their salvation. My counselor told me that the Bible says heaven is perfection, so if my version of heaven would not be perfect without my pets, then they would be there with me. This may have been a simple answer to give a young girl, but it comforted me. It wasn't until I started thinking about it later that it gave rise to different thoughts. I don't believe that I will have this body in heaven; rather I think my soul, my energy, goes there. Would my dog still be a dog there? In a dog body? Or would her essence, her energy, be there? Obviously, I don't think anyone can prove or know these things for sure, but I do think it's awesome to consider the possibilities.

I think it's interesting that most people feel we are quite superior to animals. Our pets seems to demonstrate unconditional love better that most people. Do you think there's a moment of omnipotence that occurs when we return to our spirit form? It would be ironic to learn that animals were more conscious than we ever gave them credit for. It's like us humans to be arrogant and believe ourselves the center of it all and the top of every food chain until we are proven otherwise. Galileo was threatened with death and imprisoned when he postulated that we on Earth are not the center of the entire universe but only a part of the system that revolves around the sun.

Some people believe heaven and hell are physical places. I know I believed this for years before actually giving it more thought. Could that be another plane of existence, dimension, or just farther up and down that we have yet to discover? Others believe that heaven and hell are what we're creating with our lives here on this planet. Is there a karmic ladder that acts like the law of attraction on a universal scale? Does our soul age or grow as we learn, or are we ageless?

What happens when we reach the top of our evolution? Perhaps we become excited to start the process over after an eon or two, or maybe we enjoy helping others in some way. I wish I had all the answers on how and why the universe works the way it does, but I'm sure there's a reason why I don't.

Before Philip and I were married, the issue of religion naturally came up. I was raised in a Methodist church until I was eight and then was baptized in and attended a non-denominational Christian church until I reached adulthood. He, as I have mentioned, was raised Catholic and was an altar boy at that. I told him from the beginning that I would attend Mass with him and would raise our children in that faith as long as anything taught was open for discussion, and I could express my thoughts and opinions. When I got pregnant with Anica, I realized that I really didn't know much about the church. I enrolled in the RCIA (Rite of Christian Initiation) class to learn more. It was a wonderful experience, and I realized that the Bible is incredible and complicated. The monsignor and instructor both held degrees in theology and were definitely more educated than I am. It wasn't until later that I actually wondered who taught them and how that person *knew*.

The priest inspired me to look at parts of the Bible and consider them differently. He helped me no longer feel fear from the book of Revelation, and he suggested when reading the Bible, we might consider the commonly held beliefs (like the earth being flat) and the scientific knowledge of the time that it was written. I had never considered things like that before.

I remember Monsignor asking in class, "Parables, like Jonah and the whale: true or made up?" I had to admit again, I really had no idea. He said they were stories Jesus used as an example and were fictional. But isn't that the ultimate point? Each person, church, or religion might answer that question very differently, just like we each load the forks in the dishwasher in our own way.

One of the biggest influences the Monsignor had was when he spoke of divorce in a Mass I attended. He started by saying that no matter what side of the pulpit you were on, this was a hard eulogy. He addressed a passage from the New Testament where Jesus had told a man that getting a divorce was wrong.

My brother had told me "God hates divorce" two days after I filed for divorce in my first marriage. At first I didn't even believe that was in the Bible, but he assured me that Malachi 2:16 said just that. I looked it up, and there it was, adding a layer of guilt and judgment when I was already feeling so hurt, empty, and vulnerable. I felt such incredible loss and sadness at this time, and his statement played on my insecurities. I didn't truly feel like God was angry with me; I believed that I was supposed to create a life where I could be happy, but his comment left room for a small feeling of doubt in those early days after my divorce.

It was a decade later when monsignor said, "Let me explain why Jesus said that and what I think he meant." I listened quite attentively, and before long unexplained tears wouldn't stop streaming down my cheeks. I guess my brother's words hurt me more than I had realized.

He explained Jesus's message as noted in the New Testament of Mark 10:1–8. A Pharisee (a person belonging to one of the different branches of the Judaism religion of that time) had asked Jesus about divorcing his wife. He'd wanted Jesus to tell him it was fine. In those times a divorced woman and all their children were cast out of the man's home and left to become homeless beggars or prostitutes. He explained that often the wife's family would try to help her, but usually with seven to twelve children in tow, they rarely could afford to take them in. She might be returned the dowry that she brought when she married, but that was it. No alimony, child support, or education, and the men were free to forget that wife and their children ever existed. Jesus was explaining to the Pharisee that his wife and children were a part of him, not separate, and he must consider this when making these decisions.

I think that Jesus meant for us to employ this logic in all relationships. Turn the other cheek; if a man takes your shirt, given him your jacket as well; etc. If you considered everyone a part of yourself, you wouldn't let someone else go cold or hungry if it were within your power to help. You would help feed or clothe a stranger, just like you would feed and clothe yourself or your child. What would our world be like if we considered everyone a brother or sister, son or daughter? Realizing that we are all one, a part of each other, and interconnected on a level greater than this physical plane made an enormous difference in my frame of mind. It changed how I felt about war and a whole multitude of topics. With that whole biblical frame of reference, Jesus's statement to this man is more understandable. It also shows how the underlying meanings in the Bible can be viewed so differently as we each look at the words through our own filter of experiences.

Trust your intuition as the truest measure of the truth and not what someone else would tell you the truth is.

- The Bible (and *Star Trek*) tells us that God has many names: Jehovah, Emmanuel, Alpha, and Omega. Can we also add Life, Universe, and Collective Energy? Are you still you no matter what label we give you? Is God still God?

- Try reading your favorite biblical passage and play around by exchanging the word *God* for one of these: *Universe*, *Life*, *Peace*, *Freedom*, or *Love*.

- What if we are connected to all there is, no matter if you call it God or collective consciousness? What if you could tap into that anytime you wanted and you made time to do that? Some pray, some meditate, some sing, some dance, some open their arms and picture a bright light connecting their heart to the cosmos, some pour themselves into the music of their instrument, others may do that with a sport or by being in nature. Does one of those move you? How? What if you consciously tried to be open and feel part of it? Would that change your life?

- Is one type of worship more powerful than another? Are they parts of a whole or different? Are the prayers of different faiths received differently by the divine? Do you suppose they could all be same, like different colors of the same rainbow? Do you think it matters if you choose one or your partner chooses another?

- Is it possible there could be experiences or lessons for us to learn from non-human forms? Could you imagine the wondrous delight of a bird's flight or the peacefulness of a giant sequoia swaying in the breeze protecting many different little creatures beneath your branches?

- I listened to a minister one time talk about the theory of evolution versus the theory of creation, and he said, "Why can't they both be true?" Why do we feel like we have to choose the black or white when looking at issues like this?

# Notes

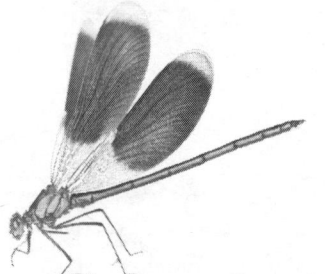

# Control and the Mirror

I'm not sure why the election of 2008 was so big for me. I usually remain a little casual and aloof about politics, but for some reason I felt strongly that year. For weeks I had been seeing "YES on PROP 8, Restore Marriage, Restore Family" signs crop up, and they rubbed me wrong. A yes on proposition 8 created a state constitutional amendment banning marriage between same-sex couples.

Fifteen years ago I probably would've said that there should be a wedding ceremony for straight couples and a civil ceremony for gay couples. Is there any difference between our souls? Is Straight or gay any different than white or Hispanic, male or female, rich or poor? It's a label to describe our experience in this life, in this body only. If you Google "biology and sexual orientation," you will see a barrage of articles and research data. Most of it expresses that there are genetic and hormonal differences between those that are heterosexual and homosexual. I know that some people will still maintain it's a choice, and maybe it is. I choose to write with my right hand. It comes easier and more natural, as I am genetically predisposed to being right-hand dominant. Yes, when I broke my arm in second grade, I managed to write with my left handed for a few weeks, but it felt awkward and wrong. What if the whole concept of homosexuality is as easily described as some of us are right handed and some are left handed? Whether God chooses for us or we get to choose for ourselves, it must be the brave and adventurous souls who come to this life in a body that is gay, physically, or mentally challenged. You've got to be courageous to be different in our society.

I wonder why these issues become such spiritual and political hot spots. Can you imagine saying that left-handed people can't marry or treating them like they are second-class citizens? Can you imagine being left phobic? Hopefully someday we can look at all people and see difference, like sexual orientation, the way we now see blood types: some of us are type O+, some A or B-. None are better, they are greater than 99 percent the same. What if being left handed or gay goes back to being part of a soul plan?

I think we would be wise to remember that at one time in our not so distant history we burned many innocent people at the stake, convinced that they were witches and the cause of sickness and disease. Today we know better and understand about viruses, bacteria, and immunology. Why do you think we persecute the things we don't understand?

There were several other ballot propositions besides proposition 8 being voted on Tuesday, November 4. There was the passage of a high-speed rail train, a bond measure to build and update children's hospitals, a measure to improve the conditions for livestock and farm animals, and two clean energy bills. I turned on the news and watched Barack Obama slowly win the electoral votes and be named the upcoming president of the United States. Both he and John McCain gave wonderful, passionate speeches, and I was thrilled that our country had come far enough to look past color and elect our first African American president and yes; I will be excited to see a woman hold office at that level too.

As the night went on, the remaining election results bothered me. The proposition on farm animals won easily, but the children's hospital barely squeaked by. On the way to bed Philip said, "It's crazy. People care more about animals than they do the children of our state!" The high-speed rail passed, proposition 8 was narrowly passed, and there was a barrage of people on TV talking about how great it was that the sanctity of marriage was restored. It was? How? Our local political analysts bickered. One side said he worried when we started taking rights away from people. He remarked that he was pretty sure the constitution meant equal rights for *all people*, not just straight people. His opponent flippantly shrugged and said, "Well, people can't have everything they want."

Both clean energy bills were defeated, despite the fact that my city is in the top three for the worst air quality in the nation as rated by the American Lung Association. The AQI (Air Quality Index) is part of every news broadcast and often varies between unhealthy for sensitive groups, our children, elderly, or sick and unhealthy for everyone. I went to bed feeling so disappointed in my own state, and I woke up feeling the same way.

The next morning Anica's mood seemed to mimic my own. She was definitely having a rough morning by any six-year-old standard. I told her to comb her hair and brush her teeth "for a good two minutes," not because she doesn't usually brush well but because I felt grumpy. When her little brother brushed for a few seconds and announced "Done!" she began to get angry about the lack of equality. From my bedroom I heard her telling him, "Lucas Brant, you brush your teeth better than that. You need to brush longer!" He refused to do that and with her temper clearly rising, she started to lecture him.

"Anica, speak with respect, please, and remember you're not his mommy," I called from my bedroom. I heard a loud and frustrated groan as I walked to the bathroom. The similarity between our situations suddenly seemed so clear. We both wanted someone else to think and act the way we did. We both had compelling arguments as to why the other parties should do it our way, and we both felt really frustrated that things weren't going the way we wanted them to.

I took a deep breath and entered the bathroom. I asked Lucas to give us a minute, and she began to justify her case. I told her, "I understand. No, I really,

really understand. You're frustrated and angry. You wanted Lucas to do things your way, and you know what? I feel the same way this morning." I pointed to my reflection in the bathroom mirror, "That's the only person who can do what I want them to. I can hope that other people will see things my way. I can argue why they should. But I can only get that person"—pointing again—"to do things my way." We each had to decide if we wanted to be grumpy or let it go and be happy. "That's also the person who can really make me happy and decide to make it a great day," I told her. We told our reflected selves that we were going to choose a great day. I remembered that we (meaning all souls) are exactly where we are supposed to be. That doesn't mean we can't grow, can't choose to be open or closed, but that we are each where we are for a reason. We are all going to perceive things differently, and having people on opposite ends of these topics makes it easier for us to decide how we feel. We are all likely to label things as right or wrong to fit within our own frame of reference and experiences and that's okay. I cannot force, cajole, manipulate, or convince others to see any part of life my way, and I wouldn't really want to.

- What if we worried about ourselves and not our neighbor? I read a quote by Albert Einstein that said, "What other people think about you is none of your business." It seems, at some point in our life, we spend a great deal of energy worrying about what someone says or thinks about us. Why is that?

- Does what someone says or thinks about you diminish you in some way? Does it alter who you are at a soul or cellular level? If you could let things like this go, would it change a work relationship?

- We often have strong opinions of others but would be embarrassed to share our thoughts about them to their faces. Why is that? Is it because we would want more respect or slack given to us if the situation were reversed?

- How much power do people have over you? How much of that is real, and how much of that is the power that you give them?

# Notes

# The Scum

Think about a small child or a baby whom you care about. What are they doing developmentally? Drooling? Sitting? Walking? If they are older, maybe they are learning body parts or letters. They all cry a lot, no doubt; they all will have tantrums as they struggle to express themselves. Their world is very narrow because as children they have little control of their surroundings, and part of their development is thinking only about their life, their immediate wants and needs.

Do you become angry with that child because they can't perform long division? Do you punish the four-year-old who doesn't understand physics? Of course not. We look at them and say, "You're not there yet, but as you grow we will teach you those things." Maybe our souls are the same way. When I read about great spiritual leaders, like Buddha, Jesus, the Dalai Lama, Dr. King, Gandhi, Mother Theresa, it seems that they had a certain wisdom about them. They didn't get hung up in pettiness or the illusions of this lifetime. They were able to let it go when they had been hurt or their life didn't turn out the way they had planned. All gave messages of peace, love, and helping others as keys to a fulfilling life. Even at different biological ages, they seemed wise and like old souls. I don't think you can rush this process anymore than you can rush to get from one to five. It takes time, physical growth, developmental growth, and the experiences you get at two, three, and four prepare you to be five. Besides, it's fun to be all those ages. We learn so much, and we teach those older and younger than us along the way too.

It's easy to look at people with distaste and think, *What scum!* When we watch the news and see people who randomly hurt someone else, especially a child, it's easy to see them as evil or bad. We may want to lock them away or do violent things back to them in the name of justice. There are people who commit tremendous atrocities that seem to scream *evil* to our very core. Take a deep breath and stand back for a minute. Instead of getting wrapped up in the hatred of them, what if we considered them as children or young souls who need to grow? Do you believe that any soul plans to come to this life to be bad? Is it possible that we need someone to play the villain once in a while? Would the main characters of any story ever learn anything or grow without the antagonist? Again, I don't have all the answers, but I think the questions are worth considering.

Is it possible that some people are caught up in the illusion of power, greed, or fear and that contributes to acts of anger or violence? I know I've had moments where I've been clouded by those very illusions, and I've acted in ways I'm not proud of.

Maybe your soul is in middle school, so things that seem easy and common sense to you are struggles to those in preschool. Think about all the things that are easy for a seventh grader: reading, writing, socializing, knowing their parents' version of right from wrong, balance, running, holding their attention for thirty-plus minutes. How overwhelming and impossible would any of those tasks be for a three-year-old? Could our spirit or soul have developmental stages too?

Do you think they will evolve, grow, and perhaps choose to experience the flip side of themselves in another lifetime? Do you think you got to middle school without first being in preschool too?

Of course there must be consequences for people who hurt others or break the law. Sometimes I try to imagine our society 1,000 years from now. Will we have come up with solutions other than prisons? Will we have found a way to lower the incidence of violent acts and make prisons more effective? Will we have a whole new approach? How would a highly evolved society handle these issues?

I believe that we're slowly growing as a society. We've changed the bar of what's an acceptable form of punishment. We no longer stone to death someone who has an affair, and most states no longer use corporal punishment in school. We are beginning to evaluate if certain crimes are more effectively treated with therapy and rehab than jail time.

There seems to be a big willingness of enormous groups of people to re-evaluate. A spiritual movement is going on to consider things like the law of attraction, looking at a new spirituality versus the old, and seeing things from more open and different perspectives. There are entertainment shows on primetime making things like psychic abilities seem like a gift instead of a curse.

Thanks to the "go green" movement, most people can finally acknowledge that our actions affect our environment. We are beginning to see how we are a part of the planet. It seems ironic and a little backward that we can connect to the planet before we can connect to each other. In the end it makes no difference; we are all one.

- What if all souls were a brilliant flame? Is one more brilliant than another? Is any soul less brilliant than another? Think of a famous person who seems dynamic and smart. It could be the President or Oprah or Miley Cyrus if you're closer to Anica's age than mine. Do you think they have celebrity status as a spirit? Is your soul as beautiful as theirs or Mother Theresa or a gang member or prison inmate? Do you think they still play that role in the afterlife? What about the spirit in a crippled body, the man with HIV, the child with Downs, the baby with cerebral palsy?

*Forks in the Dishwasher*

- Pretend you didn't believe you were a part of something greater than yourself and believed yourself to be insignificant. You also felt that you must fight for everything in your life and are deeply caught up in the illusion of power. You believe if you show your power over others that you will finally be something greater than what you are. If you were raised in that environment, would your personality be drastically different? How would you act differently?

- What if we taught our children and emphasized, "We are all one" is just as important as math or foreign language? Would our world look and feel differently? How?

# Notes

# Death

Some people are so afraid of death. Most people I have met agree that there's life after this body. They may think of it as traditional heaven and hell. Others may believe in a universal consciousness to which we all reconnect. In my life I've only met two people who said they felt we were like a light switch that simply turned off and ceased to exist. Scientifically, it seems well supported that our energy must go somewhere. Ice cubes melt to water and water boils into steam, but we don't deny that the steam is there. Can we be simpler than a glass of water?

As I reflect back to my mom's death, it wasn't obvious to me at the time, but she tied up all her commitments into a nice tiny bow. She ended a term as president of a women's Christian organization and quit her job of ten-plus years. She had planned to apply for a different district but didn't quite get it done. She had lost that last ten pounds she struggled with for so long. That same summer she developed a slight cough and pain in her chest when she exercised.

My sister had a dream that our mom had died. She picked up our mom the next day, saying she wanted to take her for ice cream and took her to the urgent care instead. A chest X-ray showed something in her right lung. The physician put her on a ten-day course of antibiotics and scheduled a re-check. I remember feeling scared when I heard it could be pneumonia or TB; somehow my twelve-year-old self sensed it was serious. That week I had a dream of my own. It was rare that I could "see" in a dream, usually I have a sense of knowing, but nothing like watching TV. In this dream I could see we were going through my mom's clothing and belongings after her death. We were laughing and having fun as we sorted through clothes and told stories. I woke up mortified. I would certainly not be laughing and enjoying myself if I'd just lost my mom. I felt weird and guilty but had no one to talk to about it.

The re-check chest X-ray showed no improvement. The physician explained she would need a bronchoscopy, a procedure where a scope is advanced into the lungs to visualize and take a sample of the tissue or fluid. This identified the problem, a rare type of lung cancer—alveolar cell. Unfortunately she had a complication (pneumothorax) during the procedure, and her lung collapsed, letting the cancerous fluid into her chest cavity. Her doctor said she had about three months to live, and with chemotherapy it might extend her life to five years. She wanted to rely on her faith to heal her; Dad wanted her to do every treatment possible. I think he felt an overwhelming urgency to make up for the years of poor communication and marital discord. In the end it didn't matter.

Ten days later, on her second day of chemotherapy, she threw two blood clots. Any type of blood clot can be serious. When clots reach a small blood vessel, they occlude it, preventing the surrounding tissues from getting oxygen. These clots can go anywhere, but if they go to the brain, lungs, or heart can cause considerable injury. If the clots are tiny, they can be treated, but a big clot to these areas usually causes immediate death. The first clot was small, but the second was large, which caused her to go into cardiopulmonary arrest. As my mom coded, it was interesting that her three children were all away with people who loved them and would take care of them. Her best friend, Brenda, had taken me back-to-school shopping. Mom had insisted that my sister go to the beach for the weekend with her husband, and my brother was with his wife and seven-month-old daughter in another city. My sister had laid down to take a nap and began to dream. She saw our mom's hospital room with doctors and nurses working franticly. At the end of the bed, she saw my mom standing close to a spirit, and she was saying, "Stop. It's okay. You can all stop, I'm home." She heard someone crying from a distance and moments later saw our dad in the hallway crying as the code continued. The phone woke her up, and her husband brought her the news—Mom had died.

Two days later Brenda and I went through my mom's belongings. It was in a different room than my dream had shown, but we happily joked and told stories. We talked about her clogs that she used to kill the snails in her garden, the fake cheetah print coat, and a checked orange suit. We giggled about the funny clothes, told stories about days we were reminded of, and I snuggled with some of her softest sweaters. I knew it was okay that we were laughing. I didn't feel awkward or guilty. Neither my sister nor I have had many dreams like that since. But I've had many experiences where I knew she was telling me she was with me.

When she first died, I felt physical pain for a while. It was like there was a shredded, empty hole inside my chest. Then, I'm sure to cope, I began to feel numb—no sadness, no tears, just nothing. Everyone said the exact same thing to me, "Oh, I'm so sorry." It was usually followed up with, "If there's anything I can do, just let me know." After twenty or thirty times, I began to get angry. Did anyone think they were as sorry as I was? All the flowers died, and where did all those people go? All their notions of "Anything I can do..." and they had all disappeared. Only my mom's best friend remained connected to me. My father, going through his own grief and struggles, managed to alienate my sister and push others away even more.

I was angry with God. It took a while to get through those stages of grief and years to not feel sad and lonely. It was probably ten years before I could be grateful that she died in a quick and painless way and did not feel cheated out of that promised three months to five years. It was also about that long before I began to realize that all the events of my life were a tapestry. Each thread of my fabric had meaning and purpose to allow me to grow, experience, and choose. My parents were my parents for a reason. I chose them in order to have a specific experience. I wouldn't have become the person I am without those events. Do I wish she were still here? Sure. Do I wish she could give me a hug, be at my kids' birthday parties, have attended my wedding? Of course I do. I think we all long to have people in human form. Mostly it's a lot easier to hear them and feel them hug you back.

From my own experiences, I respected the grieving process as being a very personal journey. As a nurse, I realized that there wasn't much I could say to families after their loved one died. I could assure them their loved one wasn't in pain, wouldn't be scared, that I would be with them and offer to call family or clergy. By and large the biggest part of the journey was his or her own. I wrestled whether to say, "I'm sorry," remembering how offensive I had found those words. But what else was there to say?

After a few years in the ICU, I saw patients on the edge of death linger for days beyond what should be possible. At times they were waiting for someone to travel from another state and get to their bedside. Then once their loved one had arrived, they would pass within minutes. I saw one woman whose family held vigil at her bedside for days, waiting for her death, and she must have known they shouldn't watch. After nearly a week of someone constantly at the bedside we asked they step out for five minutes. We suggested they get coffee from the cafeteria while we sneak in, give her a bath, linen change, and much-needed shampoo. Twelve or so family members shuffled out of the room toward the door. They had just walked out when her heart rate began to drop off. We sent someone to try to grab them before they got to the elevator but didn't make it. Over two minutes she went from a heart rate in the eighties tapering down gently... seventy-four... sixty-eight... sixty-two... fifty-four... forty-seven... thirty-two... twenty-one... ten... gone. We called them overhead to come back to the ICU, but her pulse was gone by the time they got back. I worried they would be angry, but they were relieved. A family member later said that she knew she would have gotten hysterical watching, even though it was expected.

I began to see a pattern over and over. Each spirit knew when it wanted to go, and that's when it happened. I tell new nurses not be upset when a patient dies on their shift. I explain, "It's because their spirit knew you would take care of their family. They knew it was all right to go with you. You have to realize it's really a great compliment."

I don't know exactly when I stopped believing in coincidence and luck. But it didn't take long as a nurse to realize that no one dies before his or her time. I believe even things that appear accidental or tragic were planned before that soul ever came to this body and this lifetime. It was part of the experience they were destined to have. Whether you were going to be here for three days or one hundred and three years, I think you knew and understood the purpose and gift of this life before it even began. I know it feels so tragic when a young person dies, but I can't help but think that they must be remarkable souls to have finished their life's work or soul's plan so quickly. I look at how my mom tied up all those loose ends, how the writing changed in her journals, and it seems clear her spirit knew she would be going home soon, even before getting that cough.

When my children were young, I remember thinking, *Should I teach them what I have learned? Maybe I shouldn't go there.* I felt concerned that my beliefs were no longer "mainstream." One night Anica said that she hoped that if I came back later in her life she would recognize me. She was five, but I understood what she was concerned about and reassured her. What if they went to school and talked about things in terms of "this lifetime?" I felt concerned but also thrilled that she was open to the universe and to big ideas and concepts. I remembered she chose to be my daughter for the experiences and beliefs I would share with her and that we would learn together. They understand that we're spirits having a human experience, and I hope it helps them someday when they need to cope with the stages of life and death.

I know this leaves a few issues in the air, like what happens after death. And what about suicide? I can only tell you my best guess. My thoughts on these issues come from reading and listening to different people, and all I can say is that these are the parts that "felt true" to me.

I don't think that anyone commits suicide lightly. Occasionally it might seem impulsive, but it comes when someone feels desperate, trapped, and horribly sad. I don't think any spirit, angel, collective consciousness, or God condemns them or judges them. It seems an unfortunate choice because certainly there will be a wake of hurt, pain, and unexplored options left behind that they couldn't see through their pain. I think that in each lifetime our soul has things it wants to experience, feel, explore, or even learn. If one cut short the experience here, wouldn't it be likely we'd still want to have that specific experience and need to try again? Could we all have lifetimes when we get caught up in the illusions and feel like there's no way to solve our problems? Haven't we all done poorly on a test or set a goal that we didn't reach? Perhaps suicide isn't much different than that on a soul level. Obviously, for those left behind on our human plane, there's much pain and loss to deal with and work through.

As far as what happens when we cross to that other plane of existence, I believe that we're met by souls who love and care for us. I've had too many patients who began to see and talk to deceased family members or friends in the last hours or days of life. I remember very early in my career I had a patient go on and on about "the light." It was before I felt completely comfortable with the subject of death and realized what a compliment that was. I told him, "I'm going to hope you're talking about the X-ray viewer!" I tried to ignore the fact that the viewer was on the other side of the room.

- What if we realized that we're all really just renting space on this planet? Do we get a sense of status from the stuff we claim as *mine*? We pay to have storage units to house extra stuff that we don't even have room for.

- What if all your belongings were lost in a fire, earthquake, hurricane, tornado, or tsunami? What if you had been born and raised in Gaza and were escorted from your land and house after boundary lines changed? We get a lot of comfort from the equity in our house, our retirement funds, and the money in our bank account. Those industries can collapse, do collapse, and will likely collapse again. Are we any less valuable? Are our souls damaged? Perhaps just our egos are lost. Do they provide the type of security we think they will?

- Suppose our soul has a plan for this lifetime. Could the things we chalk up to coincidence, luck, or fate be reminders we've arranged for ourselves? If not from us, could they be sent by angels, our spirit guides, or loved ones?

# Notes

# Living Awake

I felt like I'd been living awake and conscious for a long time. By that I mean being an active participant in life, choosing the things I wanted to focus on in myself, and my life. I wasn't just letting life happen to me and feeling like I had no control over it. I believed in the law of attraction, intention-setting, and my own spiritual path felt open and expanding. I was totally unprepared for the way my next realization would come. My niece, Tegan, visited one weekend and, as usual, was reading a book. She had just finished the novel and offered it to me to read.

"It's very good," Tegan offered in a coaxing way.

"No…" I hesitated. I wasn't sure I wanted to read a novel. Most of my recent reading had been spiritual, inspiring, or enlightening. Each had in some way made me really think. I'd enjoyed that sense of growing and felt reluctant to read a "novel." I almost felt like it would be a waste of my time.

"Are you sure? It's really good," she said.

I said "no" again, and Tegan didn't push. A month later while volunteering in Lucas's kindergarten classroom, the teacher and another mom brought up this same book. Both passionately told me it was excellent and recounted a few things they loved about the characters. Lucas's teacher asked, "Do you want to read it? I'll bring it for you?"

I wish I could say that I'd had an "aha" moment and realized that perhaps there was something for me to learn here but it was a human moment where I was clueless. My thought is, when different sources are suggesting the same idea or book, maybe take the time to stop and consider it.

I remained a little reluctant to reading outside my recent genre, but eventually, I gave in and said I would read the romantic novel that Tegan and the others had suggested. If you believe in coincidence, you might say it was just a popular series, and that's true too. However, I learned that insight can be found in places you might never expect. I borrowed the book from Lucas's teacher and was totally amazed when I felt obsessed to devour not just that book but the entire series. When I finished I had trouble for a few days not thinking about the story. The characters feel incredible intensity and passion for each other, but they are also self-sacrificing and truly seem to love unconditionally. They have many, many obstacles and personal flaws they must overcome in the books.

I loved the stories, but realized they had left me depressed with a sense of dissatisfaction in my own life. For a few days I kept thinking about the characters, feeling a longing for something they had. Different parts of the story would play out in my head; I was even tearful. They had money, no time constraints that make life hectic-feeling, like mine sometimes did; they had a sense of grace, and certainly all the characters had amazing physical beauty, but it felt like there was more to it than that.

It was a few days before I could articulate what was going on in my head. In the book they lived so awake. They didn't say, "Love you," in passing as one walked out the door or turned over to go to sleep. If they said "I love you," then they made eye contact, touched the other's face, and felt the love as they said it. All of their relationships were "alive." I was sad, realizing that at that particular moment most of my "I love yous" were absently attached to "goodbye" as someone hopped out the door or when I hung up the phone. When was the last time I had really felt it throughout my body as I said the words? It had been a while. When had I last told my children both how amazing they were when they were still and listening?

I talked to my friend Kris about the loose, tangled thoughts in my head and my conclusions. She said, "Maybe this is the next part of growth for you—to realize and decide to be more awake." It hadn't occurred to me until she said it. I sat in the parking lot of the hospital with tears running down my face as we talked, not wanting to walk inside. I wondered, perhaps this was what I needed to wake up that daily facet of myself. I've said to friends before, "It's all about the small stuff." And that's the part I was longing for—the moments of intensity combined with awareness. We get so distracted by the laundry, the messy house, the business, running to swim class, and dance that we forget to be present in our relationships.

Multi-tasking is an admirable skill, but it doesn't help you much when you are trying to be present in anything. When was the last time I'd given Philip my total attention when he walked in the door and asked, "How was your day?" Usually I asked while I was wiping off the counter or opening the mail.

For a week or two I felt lost. I wanted that feeling back in my life. I started with what I could do and give. When I spoke to Philip, I made eye contact. I touched his face when I kissed him. I said and felt "I love you" in my mind when the words left my mouth and when we kissed. His response was staggering. It was as though he had awakened with my tiny bits of focused energy. We began to talk deeply and passionately again. Within days we seemed so in sync, like our spiritual, sexual, and intellectual energies were on the same level. It was incredible the way our relationship felt when we were really present for it. I began to be more "present" with my children and take even a few moments to connect instead of drone on about being late to school, getting homework done, or taking a bath. Their response was there too. They were calmer and they listened more to me. I was able to take things in stride, and see the humor in things. I felt more peaceful and empowered. I started saying to myself, "I have plenty of time," instead of worrying about getting out the door.

Kris and I wrote out a list of what we really were choosing for our lives. I asked myself, "How am I going to stay centered, awake, and feeling like I am in this moment?" How do we keep ourselves operating on that higher plane where we're being the greatest version of ourselves? I can only share what I do.

Keep reading and keep listening. Give yourself a moment to take a deep breath or have a minute of stillness every day. Leave yourself reminders: the welcome message on your phone, the note on your computer, a Post-it on the dash, and, after a few weeks when those things become part of the scenery, change them up. Make a promise to yourself: "When I hear this song, when I see these things, I will stop, refocus, take a breath, and concentrate for a moment." Make a point to cultivate a friendship or two with someone who thinks the way you do, who can give you encouragement, and help you stay positive when you need it. Ask the universe at large to give you a nudge when you need to get on track. I heard of a woman who asked the universe to trip her when she needed to refocus. Whenever she stumbled, she smiled because she took it as a reminder. I'm not sure I would ask to trip, but be creative.

I already told you that my thing is dragonflies. They remind me of my power to bring things to my life, to be grateful, to stop for a moment, take a breath, and appreciate what is around me.

- What if you had your own personal tricks for staying in that higher state of mind? What if when the funk/busyness/stress of life hit you, you had a way to turn it around? (We call this finding your rainbow polka-dots, in my house.) Anica can be pouty, angry, sad, or just plain negative, but put the iPod on her, and within two minutes there is joy in her eyes, voice, and heart.

- Could you pay attention for a few days and make a list of your rainbow polka-dots? What if you then incorporated them into your day, every day? Is it writing, looking at photos, a specific memory that you could recall?

- How much time do you devote to your hobbies like tennis, video games, phone calls, scrapbooking, and blogging? Could you re-direct five minutes a day to practice breathing, being still, and feeling the energy around you? What do you think you would learn about yourself?

# Notes

# Balance

The best part of *your* spiritual path will be that you see your thoughts validated and the information that God/spirits/angels/life (pick the term you like best) is giving you will be repeated again and again. It can be through different books, music, the show that pops up on TV, the wrong link on the computer that takes you to somewhere very interesting, or the angel friend who says exactly the thing you need to hear. Each time you hear those things, the old will be confirmed and a tiny new piece will be added. The messages will come from everywhere outside you, and then there will be those thoughts of inspiration that occur inside your head alone. Don't discount them. If you chalk them up to a coincidence or let yourself believe that you "got lucky," then the message is "I don't believe."

I expect your path to take you places mine never did, and, by all means, never feel like you have to see things exactly my way. I didn't write this because I have all the answers. Does anyone have all the answers? I don't think so. For me, it's wonderful, mind-blowing, and empowering to go down this path to learn, be open, and consider new perspectives.

Yes, I still get bogged down with life and sometimes forget to take the moments I need to feel centered. As soon as I notice, I start with the pieces that have always worked for me. I write or say some "I am…" statements. My friend Kris usually senses something and starts to send me positive text messages for a week, and, within a few days, I'm excited and curious again. Where will my next big thought come from: a song, a book, a dragonfly, or a stranger? Maybe not knowing is part of the excitement.

I think most nurses would tell you, if you have an unusual heart rhythm and ask seven different cardiologists to look at it; they will give you seven different answers.

Does that help to remind you of the most important lesson? Whether you are talking about EKGs, biblical interpretation, world politics, ways to grow spiritually, or how to solve a problem, there is definitely more than one way to look at it and do it. There is also more than one way to load the forks in the dishwasher. Isn't it all really a balance? Finding your own path while being open, being able to talk about what you believe in a way that is non-threatening but still genuine. Balancing chores like getting the laundry done while finding moments to nurture your spirit, and maybe being able to see when to load the forks together and when to separate them.

It was my wish that I could take my years of reading, learning, and growing and offer it to you for consideration. I look forward to the times when my children say, "Mom, did you ever consider…" and I can have that thrill of a new idea. The next time someone approaches you with a new idea, I would encourage you to stop for a moment and consider their perspective or concept. We often discount so much in a knee-jerk reaction. What do you really believe about it? Is that what you were taught or did your experiences lead you to your conclusions? Could there be more to the topic than what you have previously considered? I hope that I never have too much pride to admit, "No, that never occurred to me!"

If this book can help you think big or touch a note inside you, then I will have served my purpose and been that positive ripple to you. I love my time on this planet. I love feeling connected and excited about learning. Maybe it's really only remembering what we are a part of. I want to inspire you: *Be an adventurer and explore!*

- Do you think that to achieve balance you need polarity? By that I mean, do you think that you need a little loss once in a while to truly appreciate and embrace all that you have? Do you need a rough patch every so often so that you can feel and notice the good? Do we need the rain once in a while to appreciate the sunshine?

- What if besides the pledge of allegiance to our country, we made a pledge to humanity and to our highest selves? How would yours start? What would you say?

- What if our children said this one in school too? What if we helped each of them follow their hearts and made up their own individual pledge? Would any changes trickle out to our communities?

# Notes

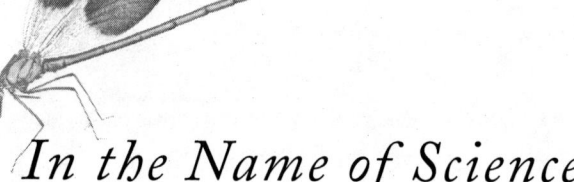

# In the Name of Science

I love to try things and proudly say, "In the name of science." Mostly it's having fun or a good excuse to try something crazy. The remainder of this book is a small collection of things to try. They may expand your way of thinking and be moving to you, or they may not. I think the fun comes from trying and being open to the possibilities. If it seems fun to try, then do; if not, then don't.

I suggest you create a note page in your computer or get a notebook to write a few lines about what happened when you tried them. I recorded what I experienced in the next chapter, but I want you to try them first and see the similarities and differences in our experiences. Don't read about my reflections until you have written your own, otherwise your experience might be altered. I'd be influencing you, or you would have an expectation. Here are a few of the exercises I have enjoyed.

1. For a few days, look in the mirror at least once a day, or every time you go to the bathroom, and say "who" or "*who*." You're posing yourself a question. See what pops into your head. Try it and see what you get out of it.

2. Really look at your body (yes, be naked) and note your thoughts. Try blessing and thanking every part of your body. As you do, consider what each part of your body does or has done for you. Try it once a day for three days and note if your feelings or reflections toward your body change over the three days.

3. During your day today close your eyes for a moment and think, *This is it*. By this I mean imagine if everything stopped now and there was only this moment. How does it make you feel? What thoughts come to your mind? Tomorrow try the same exercise, but this time, *This is it* means your last moment on the planet

in this lifetime. What thoughts and emotions come to mind?

4. When you are missing someone, especially someone who has passed away, sit or lie in a quiet spot and let pictures and memories of that person come to your mind. Focus on the details of those memories. Each thought will seem to trigger another. Allow those thoughts to flow and note how you feel. If you get lost in other thoughts, try re-focusing or wait for another time. Do not clock watch, but give yourself fifteen minutes of uninterrupted time to give this a try.

5. Try setting your intentions. Think of several things that you want to be or how you would like to be described. Write, say, and think them every day for a month. "I am_____." Whatever the "I am" statement you choose, that will be exactly right for you.

6. Have you heard that scripture, "There by the grace of God go I"? Try turning it around from the perspective that we're all one and have been

here in many different forms. Look at people all around you and when you notice them say, "There I go, being controlling again," "There I go, being a willful child again," "There I go, being a military dictator," "There I go being so kind." Notice the things you might perceive as good or bad and say, "There I go again being…" If we have all been the young and old, the nice one, the mean one, this might not be far off from the truth.

7. On a day when you have thirty minutes and a quiet place, lie down and breathe. Breathe in all of the life that is around you. As you breathe imagine the life of the universe flowing through your body. Imagine the stars funneling through you, the wind, the rain, the sunshine—all the things that pulse with the energy of life. Try to keep your eyes closed, still, and focused at your eyebrows so that you don't distract yourself by moving your eyes around under your eyelids. Now as you imagine these energies flowing through you, breathe deep and feel the energy

as it flows through your brain, heart, lungs, and to each limb. Visualize the cells of your body energized and glowing. See each part of yourself glow alive with the energy. See what you feel and don't worry about ending the experience; it will end itself.

8. Try imagining a stream of energy connecting you to God/the universe/the collective consciousness. You can imagine it as a solid, anchoring line, or a glistening beam of moving light. What information would you pull from that energy field? What questions do you want to ask? Examine how it feels to be "connected" to that.

9. Try to look at the world through the eyes of a child for thirty minutes. You can watch your own from a distance, watch story time at a library or bookstore, or just watch at a park. What do you notice about them and their interactions, their presence and their mannerisms?

10. After saying your prayers or after a moment of stillness, ask God/angels/spirits/guides/masters (pick your own) who are helping you to be the

greatest version of myself, "Please help me to remember my life plan." Note the thoughts and feeling that come to you. And the next time, try asking a new question, such as, "Please show me what to focus my energy on."

# Notes

# My Science Report

1. When I tried the "who" exercise a few times, I noticed how lifeless my eyes looked and how I didn't really identify my body as "me" so much in that moment. It truly made it seem like a shell or package, and it gave me that feeling like, "Wow! I feel how much I'm *not* this body." It was strange. It seemed like I could even look myself up and down and yet my eyes never moved. (Exercise from Walsch, *A New Spirituality*)

2. Like most people, I used to have a long list of complaints about my own body: my stomach is pudgy; my teeth should be whiter; I want to be thinner; and I don't like my hair. It's so easy to

forget that your body is not you. It's the package that holds your soul in this lifetime; that's all. It allows us great things: to experience a hug, a kiss, to feel our baby inside us, feet to carry us everywhere all the time, our skin to protect us, our hair for protection and warmth. After this exercise, I felt so grateful for every part of me. This was a shift in my way of thinking. Yes, I still do my hair, wear a little make-up, and I love it when Philip tells me I look great. I can also think about it on a higher plane and see my body for what it is, a remarkable package and tool. (Exercise mentioned in *The Secret* DVD)

3. When I think, *This is it. There is only this moment*, even if I'm squabbling with someone, it reminds me to think bigger than myself. I find myself thinking things like, *My children are so amazing. I have been so blessed. I love my family so much. I'm so grateful for my life. I've been given so much.* All those things are constantly true in my life and are what is really important. It's crazy how the little pesky things in life can take up such

dominance in our thoughts and actions, and we give them such time and energy. (Exercise from Kabat-Zinn, *Wherever You Go There You Are*)

4. I've done this one when I miss my mom. I'll focus on her face, what she looked like, and then I'll imagine her in her fake leopard-print coat, with her glasses and without her glasses. My mind will take me to how she used to let me pick out her earrings. I'll think about how I was always drawn to the pair of Mickey Mouse or the tiny dogs earrings and her teasing me. She asked if I would ever pick a pair other than those. I'll think of the powder and the perfume she used. Sometimes my hands tingle; I've had a feeling of warmth come over me and undeniably knew she was there. I have felt her so strongly like her energy was engulfing me. I usually end up with tears running down my cheeks and thanking her for the signs that she sends me.

5. This one I have done for years, but I fell in love with the idea more after the analogy of the big, universal copy machine! Initially I said, "I choose

to be strong, I choose to be honest, I choose to be humble, I choose to be compassionate, I choose to be loving, I choose to be kind." Yes, I've occasionally added things like, "I choose to be skinny." Over time I also added, "I choose to be a great wife and have a marriage that is fun, playful, passionate, and genuine." Now if you knew Philip, it would be obvious that I drew him to my life since that describes him exactly! When I found out I was pregnant, I added, "I choose to be a great mom and have lifelong friendships with my children." My lists have been somewhat fluid overtime, changing some as I grow. I said before, I started with, "I choose," but now I simply say, "I am!" (Universal copy machine from Walsch, *Conversations with God,* Book 1)

6. When I do this, it hits home to me every time that we are all one. It saps the anger or disgust I might be feeling for someone else. To look at the news and see a gang shooting and say, "There I go again, mixed up, confused." It's hard to look past the actions, past the package, and just see

the soul. Somehow this reminds me of that and makes it really easy for me to see the soul and not the activity.

7. On the day I first tried this, I laid down in my son's room because his bed always gets wonderful afternoon sun. I relaxed and let the warmth wash over me. I closed my eyes and tried to focus on the bridge of my nose under my eyelids. I inhaled and exhaled deeply. I began to let images of nature and things that seemed full of great energy come to mind. I imagined them washing through my head and through my body. I know for the first five minutes or so, nothing tremendous happened other than my respiratory rate increasing as I focused on the energy that was being pulled through me with every breath. After a while I saw a bluish light in front of my eyelids. My eyes were closed, but I saw a light. Then, rather suddenly, I felt tears rush my eyes, and I lay there, concentrating on the light and breathing. Tears streamed down my cheeks for a few more minutes, and then it

felt like I was trying to hold on to the moment, and that sense of trying to hold on to it ended it. My cheeks and my hands were slightly tingly when I realized it was over. I cannot describe it beyond that, but I felt exhilarated, like I had experienced something very special. (This exercise is a mixture of things I had read in Gilbert, *Eat, Pray, Love* and Walsch, *A New Spirituality*).

8. I do this exercise more and more. I imagine the beam of light from my heart to the heavens. I often do this as I pray, name my intentions, or as I ask that my writing flow. Sometimes I say what I'm hopeful to accomplish and ask for me to see the ways to that goal. On occasion, as I visualize myself connected to the universe, I ask that my voice and my intentions be heard loud and strong and multiplied a thousand times. When I ask for that sense of connectedness, I take a deep breath and picture myself satisfying my goals. I find that my writing comes easily and that I feel strong and empowered.

9. I watched the kids in Lucas's classroom, during story time. Usually during my volunteer hour they had center time, but this day, there was story time instead. I'm not sure why the process was altered this particular day, but I learned from it. I noticed how incredibly in the moment the kids were. They had no sense of time or urgency and found joy in every line of the story, each picture, and even the intonation of their teacher's voice. I concentrated on their faces and the enthusiasm they felt as they listened to the book. I could feel the energy from them, like a positive wave that made me grateful and happy. I thought to myself that maybe I should stop and take the time to see the world through a child's eyes more often. I could choose to find joy in the small things and be present in each moment, rather than hurrying from task to task.

10. Once, I was trying to figure out where to focus my time: my part-time nursing job, going back to school, writing children's stories, or finishing this book, which started as a letter to my

children. I had written 90 percent of it, titled it, and printed one copy to give my friend Kris. She had only read the first few chapters. The morning after asking my question of the angels/guides/God/masters, Kris called. She said, "You're never going to guess what happened last night. My stepmom came over for dinner and was watching me load the dishwasher. She asked me, "Are you sure you want to load the forks that way?" And I replied, 'You know, there's more than one way to load the forks in the dishwasher.' Let me read you a few paragraphs of something my friend wrote."

Okay guides, point taken. Thanks for making that one so clear!

# Notes

# Final Comments

I was going to list the books that I felt influenced me the most when I realized that it's far more than individual books. It was the continued learning and layering of information that the angels gave me in many different ways. These are some of the authors whose works have touched me. If you see their books, read the back and see if one seems to be intriguing or calling you. The right one will find its way to you when you are open and ready.

- Betty Eadie
- Brian Weiss
- Elizabeth Gilbert

- Rhonda Byrne
- Jon Kabat-Zinn
- Gary Zukov
- Robert Heinlein
- Wayne Dyer
- Stephanie Meyers
- Orson Scott Card
- Neale Donald Walsch
- John Edward
- James Van Praugh
- Philip McGraw
- Richard Paul Evans
- Mitch Albom
- J. Eckhardt Tolle
- Jill Bolte-Taylor
- Benjamin Hoff
- Richard Bach
- Ainsile Macleod
- Malcolm Gladwell
- Victor Wooten

Although, I choose to live as an open book, I didn't feel it was respectful for me to make that decision for others. Therefore, a few individuals' names in the book have been altered to respect their privacy.

# Notes